The Victorious Christian Soldier in Christ's Army
By Urian Oakes
with chapters by C. Matthew McMahon

Copyright Information

The Victorious Christian Soldier in Christ's Army, by Urian Oakes, with chapters by C. Matthew McMahon
Edited by Therese B. McMahon

Copyright ©2020 by Puritan Publications and A Puritan's Mind™

Some language and grammar have been updated from the original manuscript. Any change in wording or punctuation has not changed the intent or meaning of the original authors, and has been made to aid the modern reader.

Published by Puritan Publications
A Ministry of A Puritan's Mind™ in Crossville, TN.
www.apuritansmind.com
www.puritanpublications.com

All rights reserved. No part of this publication may be reproduced, stored in a retrieval system or transmitted in any form by any means, electronic, mechanical, photocopy, recording or otherwise, without the prior permission of the publisher, except as provided by USA copyright law.

This Print Edition, 2020
Electronic Edition, 2020
Manufactured in the United States of America

ISBN: 978-1-62663-369-8
eISBN: 978-1-62663-368-1

Table of Contents

Fighting in the Spirit? 4

Meet Urian Oakes 9

To the Reader 12

Chapter 1: The Text Opened 18

Chapter 2: The Doctrine 24

    Conclusion 1: 25

    Conclusion 2: 27

    Conclusion 3: 41

    Conclusion 4: 44

    Conclusion 5: 46

    Conclusion 6: 50

    Conclusion 7: 56

Chapter 3: Uses of the Doctrine 59

    Use 1. 59

    Use 2. 60

    Use 3. 61

    Use 4. 65

    First Branch of Exhortation in Ten Directions 66

    Second Branch of Exhortation 85

    Third Branch of Exhortation 86

    Fourth Branch of Exhortation 88

Other Works on Spiritual Warfare at Puritan Publications
.... 96

Fighting in the Spirit?
by C. Matthew McMahon, Ph.D., Th.D.

"If we live in the Spirit, let us also walk in the Spirit," (Gal. 5:25).

We could rewrite this sentence in Galatians 5:25 to say, "If we live in the Spirit, let us also *fight* in the Spirit." In fact, pick whatever Christian duty you would like to put there, and *walking* sums up what that word would entail. *Walking* covers everything in the Christian life. In our present case, along with studying this topic of the victorious Christian soldier in Christ's army, Oakes is going to make a link between what it means to be "in Christ" or "in the Spirit" and connect that to "fighting" as a good soldier in Christ's army. The Spirit's work is to sanctify the believer. In the work of sanctification, it is important to make note that from one's first conversion, there then extends a *continual* holiness. The Spirit enables regenerated Christians to discern good from evil, or sin from holiness. He disposes the mind to accept truth and to know what the Scriptures contain. Here the Spirit aids the Christian in expounding Scripture in order to apply that Scripture to the Christian's life and further grow in the mystical union he now has with Christ (1 Cor. 6:17). The Spirit illuminates through his indwelling presence within the individual (John 16:16; 2 Tim. 1:14; Rom. 8:9; Gal. 4:6; 1 Cor. 3:16; 1 John 4:13; Eph. 1:13). Those who are illuminated and are indwelt by the Spirit are called by the Spirit (Gal 5:18; Rom. 8:14; Ezek. 36:27). Love to God in sincere service is the principle here, and only through the power of the Spirit can there be true Christian love reflecting Christ (1 Cor. 13) to serve God and one another. This also includes the soldier's duty to *fight* for Christ, for himself, and for the kingdom of God. Love in warfare? Most assuredly.

The degree of the Christian's sanctification and ethics will differ according to the Spirit's will and right use of God's constituted means. Romans 7 gives Christians a glimpse into the real struggle in which every believer fights against sin. They sometimes lose and sometimes win; this is not the fault of the Spirit, but their fault in either trying to partially reform, or misusing the means of grace. Ultimately, they *will be* glorified and made perfect in heaven. But the Spirit of grace enables them to *fight* their way out of every temptation (1 Cor. 10:13) although believers do not always arrest that opportunity to please God and rather, they grieve the Spirit. As Ephesians 4:30 says, "And do not grieve the Holy Spirit of God, by whom you were sealed for the day of redemption."

In our Galatians text, the apostle Paul writes to call the church at Galatia back to the Gospel which they had at the first received from his preaching. In Acts 15:1 Judaizing trouble was stirring at Antioch, "certain men coming down from Judea." They were troubling people about the meaning of what justification is, looking to go back to the law instead of the fulfillment of the law in Christ. They were looking to do good things to gain justification by works, instead of by faith. Certainly, good works are to be present in the redeemed sinner, but not until justification is first declared about them by God. This certainly doesn't mean that God does not require good works from sinners, he *certainly* does, but they have no ability to perform them until they are converted because they are fallen. What Christians accomplish in their walk with God, stems from what Christ has first done *in* them by the power of the

Spirit.[1] It stems from what Christ gives them and empowers them to accomplish in the Spirit. They are enlisted in the army of Christ, and are to set forth a standard, a way of living, that follows the fruit of the Spirit, in contrast to their former works of darkness that they worked in their lost condition. The fruit of the Spirit in a Christian is set in direct contrast, opposition to the darkness of the world, where the Apostle speaks about it as the flesh *warring* against the Spirit.

Justification, rightly understood, leads to a proper sanctifying effect that produces fruit in contrast to the works of the flesh. Works of the flesh hold all kinds of wickedness in them. The Christian must valiantly fight against them. These Galatians were to walk in the Spirit. "If we live in the Spirit, let us also *walk* in the Spirit," (Gal. 5:25). Living in the Spirit is demonstrated by not only what one believes, or what one says, but by what one *does*. It is an exhortation to follow in the steps Christ has laid out in his word through the empowerment of the Spirit of grace. It is not about joining a church to join a club for the sake of fame or status. It is about walking, and it is about fighting for the glory of Christ. Walking is *part* of salvation. Without walking, one cannot be saved. If one is saved by grace alone, *they will have a faith that is not alone*. It will indeed have works; they will indeed be fighting as soldiers in Christ's army. The Spirit changes them, baptizes them, enables them to repent, enlightens them, gives them unction and power, illuminates them to the truth of the

---

[1] See my work, *Walking Victoriously in the Power of the Spirit,* for a full treatment of what it means to be victorious in Christ, and have an abundant life through him.

word of God, equips them in spiritual usefulness, enables them to pray in the Spirit, and to exercise all manner of godliness, which is here translated, *live* in the Spirit. If they are born again by the Spirit, and all those blessings accompany them, they will in turn fight as good soldiers in the Spirit. They no longer live according to the deeds of the flesh. This does not mean they are perfect, but it does mean that the overall desire of that changed Christian is to strive *towards* perfection. They fight for that, and they do not use excuses to the contrary.

If one surveys historical theology, (*i.e.* what people believed through the history of the church and why they believed it), they would find that this little phrase, "live in the Spirit" is very useful in understanding what God requires of the Christian. William Ames said, "Theology is doctrine or teaching of living to God." Peter van Mastricht further edits this and said, "Theology is doctrine or teaching of living to God through Christ." I take this one step further. "Theology is doctrine or teaching of living to God through Christ in the power of *walking in the Spirit.*" With Oakes, I would even tailor it a bit more, "Theology is doctrine or teaching of living to God through Christ in the power of walking in the Spirit, fighting valiantly against the world the flesh and the devil for the glory of Christ."

Fighting as a soldier in the power of the Spirit is the duty of every Christian who is living to God through Christ. There is a great worthiness in fighting against the works of darkness in the Spirit according to the example of Christ, to increase in holiness. "…that you may walk worthy of the Lord, fully pleasing Him, being fruitful in every good work and increasing in the knowledge of God,"

(Col. 1:10). Fighting the wickedness and sin is walking in the light, and it is a means of fellowship with God, and with the saints. "But if we walk in the light as he is in the light, we have fellowship with one another, and the blood of Jesus Christ his Son cleanses us from all sin," (1 John 1:7). Walking in the light means Christians have fellowship with God by the blood of Christ. If Christians say they love God, if they live to God, then *they will* walk in the Spirit and walk with God, and fight as good Christians soldiers under the command of King Jesus, if they are true believers.

In the midst of a fallen world, you must be *fighting* as a Christian, in the power of the Spirit, as much as you love to live or walk in the Spirit. What an odd thing it is for a wicked person to hear that your life-long goal is to walk in the sight of God in holiness, please Christ and fight valiantly in the Spirit against the works of darkness. It sounds, to them, like some comic book fantasy. But you Christian reader, know better. You must necessarily differ from wicked men, by forsaking the course of this world, and walking according to the world to come, which is walking in the Spirit. That is *pressing* into the kingdom. That is taking it by *violence*. This is *fighting* as a good Christian solider with the weapons of our warfare that are not carnal. You are men and women of the Bible; and this book commands you to walk before Christ as a soldier, dawned with the armor of God, and wielding the sword of the Spirit with skill. As Oakes will show, *It is your life.*

As a Fellow Soldier in Christ's Army,
C. Matthew McMahon, Ph.D., Th.D.
From my study, July, 2020.

Meet Urian Oakes
Edited by C. Matthew McMahon, Ph.D., Th.D.

Urian Oakes (1631–1681) was a New England divine, originally born in England in 1631 or possibly 1632. When he was a child, he left England with his father to go to Massachusetts. He graduated at Harvard College in 1649.[2]

While in America he married Ruth, daughter of a well-known nonconformist minister, William Ames. Oakes returned to England during the time of the Commonwealth, and obtained a pastorate in Titchfield. From there he was ejected in 1662. His wife died in 1669. Two years later a deputation sent over to England to find a minister for the vacant church of Cambridge in Massachusetts and chose Oakes. He commenced his pastoral labors in November of 1671, and soon after he became one of the governors of Harvard College.[3] The college was in a difficult situation owing to the general dissatisfaction of the students with their president, Leonard Hoar. The same feeling was in some measure shared and countenanced by certain of the governors, and among them was Oakes. He and other of his colleagues resigned, and, in spite of the entreaties of the general court of overseers, would not withdraw their resignation until Hoar himself vacated the presidency on

---

[2] Calamy and Palmer, ii. 280.
[3] Harvard was originally founded to raise up Gospel ministers.

March 15, 1675. The vacancy thus created was filled by the appointment of Oakes. He, however, would only accept it provisionally; but after discharging the duties of the office for four years, in 1679 he consented to accept the full appointment, and held it until his death on July 25, 1681. Edmund Calamy states that Oakes was noted for "the uncommon sweetness of his temper," and in New England he was greatly beloved by his congregation and popular with all who came in contact with him.

His writings are "The Victorious Christian Soldier," "The Sovereign Efficacy of Divine Providence,"[4] three sermons—two preached at the annual election of the artillery company in 1672 and 1676, and the third at the election of representatives in 1673—and a monody in English verse (Cambridge, 1677) on the death of Thomas Shepard, minister of the church in Charlestown. Mr. Tyler describes Oakes' one surviving effort in poetry as "not without some mechanical defects," yet, on the whole, Oakes' power, dignity, and directness raise him far above the contemporary verse-writers of New England.

---

[4] Republished by Puritan Publications: *The Sovereign Efficacy of Divine Providence,* preached September 10, 1677, by Mr. Urian Oakes, the late (and still to be Lamented) Reverend Pastor of the Church of Christ in Cambridge, and Learned President of Harvard College. Psa. 29:10, "The Lord sitteth upon the flood: yea the Lord sitteth King forever." Isa. 41:14-15, "Fear not thou worm of Jacob. I will help thee, saith the Lord, and thy Redeemer. Thou shalt thresh the Mountains." Rom. 11:36, "For of him, and through him, and to him, are all things, to whom be glory for ever. Amen." (Boston, MA: s.n. 1682).

Oakes stands out far more conspicuously above his contemporaries by the merits of his prose. In substance his sermons wholly break through any mere formalities of Calvinism. They are intensely human, alike in their treatment of moral problems and their application of scriptural examples. The preacher is throughout a vigorous moralist, full of public spirit. The style is concise and precise (as many of his theological puritan counterparts), yet free from conceits or forced antithesis, and capable of rising into real dignity and eloquence. The purity and elegance of his Latin are proved by an example preserved in Cotton Mather's "Magnalia."

For more information, see:

Savage's *Genealogical Dict. of New England*; Cotton Mather's *Magnalia*; Tyler's *History of American Literature*; Holmes's *History of Cambridge*; Peirce's *History of Harvard University*, (pp. 44–46); Appleton's *Cyclop. of American Biogr.* Volume iv, 548; Hutchinson's *History of Massachusetts*.

To the Reader

Christian Reader,

That title of the book of the wars of the Lord, (Num. 21:14) may truly be ascribed to that *best of books*, the holy Scripture, in which, accordingly, after a short account in the first pages of it, where it speaks about finishing the heavens and the earth, and all their host, the Lord of Hosts presently acquaints us with the enmity put between the seed of the Woman, and the seed of the Serpent, (Genesis 3:15). In this we find is given to us, the Word of the Lord, which has, in a sense, gone on in war between the seeds, being the very battles that have been fought in the world, for more than 5000 years. It started between the Seed of the woman, and the serpent, and has, from the beginning of it continued to this day. And where it is also, that this earth shall be the continued field and stage of war until the last day, we find in the Revelation of John the close of this bloody scene, in the Scripture's last prediction of the great fatal and final battle between the same serpent, the Dragon and his seed, against that of the Seed of the woman. The upshot of this will be the last and amazing battle, and the eternal shutting of heaven and hell, filled with the combatants respectively, for receiving their rewards or curses as a result. The day of Judgement, without a doubt, will be the day of publishing (and by sound of the last trumpet) the completed history of the whole fight from first to last. In the interim, the Lord General has his many heralds at arms, to denounce his wars, and so proclaim also his peace to the world, both by word of mouth (as by sound of a trumpet, Isa. 58:1) and by writing also, of some of whom especially it may be said, they have not "shunned to deliver the whole counsel of God," and that in the demonstration of the Spirit, and with power. And blessed be the Lord for all the alarms, lectures of war, instructions and hortatory speeches given from the Captain of our salvation by any of his commission officers, for the doubling and fortifying our spiritual watch. Israel under the law needed the priests of the Lord (concerning the silver trumpets, (Num. 10:2, 9), so that blowing them the camp might be remembered before the Lord their God, and saved from their enemies. The whole life of every Christian is that of a man of war. Here, what may tend to accomplish and help him in his heavenly military skill, and encourage him in his spiritual conflict in which that cry is still heard (as Exod. 32:26) "who is on the Lords side?" yes, in this the battle is such that he must either fight or die, and that the consequence is for no less than *eternity*. This must necessarily be *welcome* to him. So, without question, this treatise will be a watch-word and exhortation, delivered to the principal artillery company of this land, at whose request it was first published to the ear and heart of the hearer, and is now (after not a little importunity) to the eye also of the reader, from one of our leaders (Heb. 13:17). He preached this under the

Chief Leader (Heb. 2:10), Jesus Christ, who is given for a Leader and Commander to the people, (Isa. 55:4).

The purpose of this discourse is to animate each one us, as a good soldier of Jesus Christ, to endure hardness. It gives us a sure intelligence of the happy success of this divine *militia*, the blessedness of every faithful warrior, in being "more than a conqueror." And though he may seem to be overwhelmed in this or that battle, yet as to the whole war, that he shall be, yes, in the language of truth, "an overcomer," and *above* an overcomer. A Christian's victory is indeed likened to that of his Chief Commander Jesus Christ, (Col. 2:14-15), and through that blood, and infinite grace, it is a very strange and mysterious power. He is overcoming, when in appearance he may be overcome, and he is triumphing when to the view of others, he is a crucified and captive. He is as dying and behold he lives! (2 Cor. 6:9), which is an enigma, and incredible in other combats. And yet the wonder does not seem so great that he should gain such a victory over all his enemies of this world, when we consider him as one that has (with reverence as it is spoken) "conquered the Lord himself," as is said of Jacob, whom the Lord dubbed with the name of Israel, (Gen. 32:28) because as a prince he had power with God, and had prevailed. Here we also have that strange word from the Lord himself, Song of Songs 6:5, "turn away thine eyes from me, for they have overcome me." In this way they sometimes come forth, from the dust, (Isa. 52:2) and from their wrestling places of prayer, as Luther did with those of faith, "We conquered! We conquered!" and surely such as one may glory in the Lord, and through him humbly boast even as soon as he has put on his spiritual harness, because he is here well assured, by the promise, of the victory, before he even takes a swing; and for which cause partly he may be said to be "more than a conqueror."

Every victory was not celebrated with a triumph; to be *triumphant* is to be more then to be *victorious*. There were, and are the battles, in which even the victor does not have as much cause to rejoice. Of what sort may those, of them (who being not only visibly listed under the banner of Jesus Christ, but have Christ *in* them, the hope of glory, yet) by whose divisions and sidings, and warrings one against the other, through the hour and power of darkness, and temptation prevailing, the truth and peace is lost? These wars have no triumphs. And, O! that a most serious and wise consideration of their common danger from the gates of hell, and the necessity of that brotherly union to which the Lord has entailed the blessing, by way of command, even life for evermore, might cause a retreat to it, in all quarters of the spiritual camp sounded, from those hazardous and woeful pursuits! Shall the sword devour forever? Will it not be bitterness in the latter end? How will the uncircumcised rejoice?

The most warlike Christian soldier will see, one day, that he did not have any military skill, strength, courage or weapon to spare, in which to fight for Christ.

He is empowered by the Spirit, with spiritual weapons as a called, chosen and faithful follower of the Lamb. And even as Christ's enemies, (sinful self, the devil, and this evil world (all Anti-Christianism)) fight against them, they should fight back, conquer them, and not spare *them*. The severest encounters cannot be too sharp; no quarter must either be given or taken here forever. The enemy is discovered, and those stratagems of faith in the blood of Christ proposed by the reverend author of the following treatise (whose praise is in the gates) as that, be our right taking the word, that not only victory may be gained, but what is eminently transcendent. You have here (by one of the Lord's auxiliaries, who is an expert in warring the warfare of the service of the congregation (for such will the service of the ministry be found, Num. 8:24-25), sent else from afar, for our relief, (and in such a day) graphically represented to your view of the church triumphant here on earth, more than conquering while it is indeed militant. And though their ancient triumphs were appointed for the General of the army, not for the common soldiers, yet in this spiritual war, the meanest of Christ's followers shall triumph with him, and divide the spoils. An earnest specimen of this is that they are sincere and seldom acquainted with in this life. This is where there are erected in their heart and life, trophies of the lesser victories gained, and all to the glory of him, in whom, when they are weak, they are strong. This is through the power of his might, and may conclude beforehand that they are "more than conquerors," and shall abide so superlatively forever. They will receive those military arsenals which are to be distributed to all such as are faithful to death. "I will give thee (the Lord says in Rev. 2:10) the crown of life." There is the triumphant crown not only for Paul, who was a principle champion, but 2 Tim. 4:7-8, for those who "have fought a good fight, I have finished my course, I have kept the faith: Henceforth there is laid up for me a crown of righteousness, which the Lord, the righteous judge, shall give me at that day: and not to me only, but unto all them also that love his appearing," and that he would so come quickly (O! come quickly!) is the prayer of:

The least of your fellow soldiers, desirous to serve under the royal standard of the Lord Jesus,
THOMAS SHEPARD

Chapter 1: The Text Opened

"Nay, in all these things we are more than conquerors through him that loved us," (Rom. 8:37).

In these words, we do not have the apostle Paul's ovation, but triumph; not triumph only, but something I am hard pressed even to make intelligible, exhibited in the name and on the behalf of himself and all true believers. It is proclaiming and importing a more than ordinary triumph over all those enemies that oppose themselves against the progress and advancement of a Christian in his way to the fruition of the sweet fruits of the everlasting love of God in Jesus Christ. Having perspicuously, copiously, and demonstratively asserted and vindicated the illustrious doctrine of justification in a way of free grace by faith in the Lord Jesus Christ, in the beginning of this excellent epistle, (which is ingeniously described by the great Melanchthon, the *confession* of the Reformed churches). He proceeds in the sixth chapter to discourse of the fruits and consequences of it, namely, sanctification and obedience; the mortification of indwelling sin in believers, and the renovation, or rather infusion of a new principle of spiritual life and holiness. Now because this work is but immature and imperfect, and in part only transacted in this world, and there are remainders of sin in this life in the best of saints, and because grace and corruption are vigorous, active, operative principles, dwelling so near together, under the same roof, in the same soul, yes in the very same faculties, there must necessarily arise a sharp and severe war in the soul between these two neighboring and opposite natures. The particular events and successes of this are various and uncertain; but the victory is infallibly determined in the issue on the side of grace. Grace indeed is greatly beset, much encumbered and almost overthrown for various reasons. But it will certainly wrestle and recover itself out of all the dangers that threaten it.

 Now there is a double war which is commenced and waged by believers in this life: a war with the evil of sin, and a war with the evil of sufferings or afflictions so far as they would impede or oppose them in their march to heaven. Of the war with sin, indwelling sin: (the inbred, home-bred enemy, that mother of all the abominations that are brought forth in the lives of men, that adversary that is ever molesting the peace, disturbing the quiet, and endangering the condition of the people of God) the apostle discourses feelingly and at large in the seventh chapter of this epistle. There he finally adjudges the victory to grace, in its last verse, and in the beginning of the eight chapter as well. Of the war with afflictions, or the evil of sufferings from Satan, or the world, from what hand, of what kind, and howsoever conditioned and circumstanced, he discourses admirably at the seventeenth verse of this chapter and also forwards, and he comes in the procedure of his discourse to give unquestionable assurance to the good soldiers of Jesus Christ, of the full and final decision of this grand controversy, and the happy issuing of all these hazardous conflicts. It does not matter whether with sin or sufferings, they will have a glorious and absolute victory. Insomuch as having made sure of God on the side of himself and believers, he does, in his own and their name, make an open challenge, and bid defiance to all opposite and adverse powers. Verse 31, "If God be for us who then can be against us?" He bids sin, Satan, and the evil world do their worst against believers that are in this way entrenched in, and walled about with the love of God. They are, in this way fortified and defended, aided and assisted by the almighty one, the Lord of hosts. And having laid his foundation in God's predestination, and Christ's mediation, he superstructs on it, and plainly asserts the invincibleness of every sound believer, notwithstanding the relics of sin that incumber him, the temptations of Satan that molest him, and the afflictions and evils of the world that set themselves in battle array against him. He represents to us the Christian as a person that may be opposed, combated and contended with. But the Christian is never routed, run down, totally defeated or overthrown in any engagement. Now, this invincibleness of the Christian combatant, the believing champion (that in the name of the Lord defies all the hosts and armies of earth and hell that come against him) notwithstanding the remainders of sin, the greatness and unavoidableness of his afflictions and sufferings, is expressed in the following *manner:*

    1. Negatively, Verse 35, "Who shall separate us from the love of Christ?" The argument stands in this way: if nothing can separate a Christian from the love of God in Christ, then nothing can conquer him, but he is invincible. Nothing can make that woeful destructive separation. This he proves by an enumeration or induction of particulars; shall tribulation, or distress, or persecution, *etc.* Therefore, he is invincible. This negation is clearly imported in the interrogation. This is a true and useful observation, that interrogations affirmatively expressed in scripture are accustomed to carry in them the force and signification of vehement negations. The meaning of the apostle in plain terms is, that neither tribulation, nor distress, nor persecution, nor famine, nor nakedness, nor peril, nor sword, nor anything else can possibly separate a true believer from the dear love of Jesus Christ.

    2. Affirmatively, in the words of the text; in all things we are "more than conquerors through him that loved us." As if he should say, we are so far from being prevailed over by the enemies of our salvation that war against us, from succumbing under the load they are laying on us, and losing our interest in the fruits of the everlasting love of God in Christ, by reason of the opposition that is made by the Lord in our behalf, that we carry the day, and are sure of a very glorious victory.

In this verse we may remark these two things. 1. A singular privilege: and that is victory and conquest, which is illustrated and amplified, (1.) From its extent and universality, "In *all* these things." Such as he had mentioned before, or what else can be mentioned and imagined by us. (2.) From the transcendent incomparable excellency of it. "We are more than conquerors," or, *do more than overcome*. It is a victory, with excessiveness and advantage, a victory, and something more than a victory. A superlative and incomparable conquest and victory that is obtained. (3.) From the foundation of this glorious victory, or the great and only means of acquiring and obtaining it. And that is, the Lord Jesus Christ. "Through him that loved us," the apostle says. Meaning Christ, or God in Christ Jesus. (4.) From the first, grand, impulsive use of it, the first cause of this glorious victory which is infallibly obtained, and that is, "the love of God in Christ." The special love of God in his Son Jesus Christ is the first cause of these victorious achievements making the Christian "more than conquerors through him that loved us."

2. The people that are in this way privileged, or invested in this great privilege. Those that have victory and triumph ascertained to them. We are *more* than conquerors. Not only the great apostle Paul himself, that renowned warrior, and brave champion of the Lord Jesus Christ. But this is for all true believers *universally*. He ranks himself with, and discourses of believers in

general, "that walk not after the flesh, but after the spirit;" believing, justified and sanctified men and women. They are not exempted or secured from violent onsets, furious assaults, hazardous and desperate conflicts with their mortal enemies that war against their souls. But they have this admirable advantage above all other men, that they are assured of a glorious victory. The intendment of the apostle in the words is obvious, and may be drawn into this observation.

Chapter 2: The Doctrine

Doctrine: That all true believers have a transcendent, and incomparably glorious conquest and victory in all their severe engagements with the enemies of their peace and happiness, through the love of God in Christ Jesus.

Believing, justified people, through the love of God in Christ, overcome by many degrees against the enemies of their salvation, and are much too hard for them in all their sharp disputes and encounters with them. All they who have believed through grace, and are admitted into a state of justification and, acceptance with the Lord are "more than conquerors," successful and victorious beyond expression or comparison, in their combats and conflicts with their enemies (those adverse powers that war against them). They have this through divine love in Jesus Christ.

This proposition which we have laid down, as the subject of our present exercise, and which is evidently founded and comprised in the words of the text, has a large compass and a very great circumference, as you will readily apprehend. We are now entering into a very large field, and might traverse a great deal of ground, if time and strength would allow us to pace over it. We have many things before us to be discoursed for the due explication and confirmation of this observation. The way of quickest dispatch, and greatest expedition; as well as clearness, and demonstration, will be to cast all we have to say to the doctrinal part into six or seven grand conclusions.

Conclusion 1:

Every true believer is a soldier, and engaged in a warfare. I wish it were reciprocally true, that every soldier among us is a true believer; for every soldier in Christ's army *ought* to be a believer. And of all men, they are commanded to God's service, to look death and danger in the face, and carry their lives in their hands. They have need of faith and grace, and interest in the Lord Jesus Christ, and by this the condition of their souls being well secured for eternity is infallibly and universally true, for every true believer is a soldier as we consider them spiritually. The whole body of Christians that walk by faith in this lower world, the place of sin, and sorrow, and temptation, and absence from the Lord, is apt and truly called the church militant in contradistinction from that which is, the triumphant church in the highest heavens. Those that have arrived at a gate of glory have fought their fight, and finished the course of their warfare, and are out of reach from sword, or gunshot, far enough moved out of the reach of their adversaries. They are marched out of the field, and discharged from any further service, and enjoying their reward. But the people of God in this world are in a warring state and condition. The first moment that any

Chapter 2: The Doctrine

man is effectually called and converted, and savingly worked on, he is engaged on Christ's side against the world, the flesh, and the devil, taken into Christ's service, puts on his armor, and is prepared for the battle. For the graces of God's Spirit, which are infused at a Christian's conversion, are a believer's spiritual armor, (Eph. 6:13-14). Every Christian, when he is new born, is born a soldier. It is said of Goliath, the Philistine champion, that he was a man of war from his youth, (1 Sam. 17:33). But it may be truly said of the Christian champion, that he is a man of war from his birth, and neither is he a poor naked creature, as it is with the children of the first birth. But he comes into the new world in his suit of armor, armed with complete armor of proof, vested with the graces of the Spirit of Christ. He has his excellent and invincible general, the Lord Jesus Christ; and has taken his sacred military oath of fidelity and obedience to his great Lord and Captain. He also has (if there is opportunity, and he walks orderly) his command that he is listed into, the church, I mean, he walks in fellowship with believers which he is enrolled in among the members of the church-militant generally speaking. He has his banner to fight under. His banner is the love of Christ displayed for a defense to his soldiers and followers, and a flag of defiance to their adversaries, (Song of Songs 3:4). He has his arms and weapons, offensive and defensive to fight with. He has his soldierly qualifications, and military accomplishments; courage, skill, patience, hope of victory, faithfulness to, and confidence in his General, orderliness, disposition to hardship, or whatever else may be mentioned.

Every wicked man is a dead soldier. He fights against God, tries to strengthen himself, and reaches out his hand against the Almighty, and runs on his own strength and his own power, (Job 15:25-26). He fights against himself and his own soul, keeping those lusts in play that war against the soul.

The wicked put on the whole armor of the devil, that he may be able to stand against all the shocks of conscience, or encounters of the word and Spirit of God, and fight it out to the last with the infinite majesty, to the everlasting ruin of his immortal soul. But he is neither engaged in, or provided and accomplished for the holy war we are discoursing about. An unbeliever is a conquered, disarmed slave, that men in the service of the enemies of his soul, is in no condition to fight. If he begins to stir himself (through the convictions, awakenings and alarms of conscience) and to hold up his hand, or make any resistance, he is knocked down and overcome presently, and that man is a captive (as the believer is said to be more than a conqueror) and a vassal and drudge to his own lusts, and other enemies then before. But a believer is a man of war, a soldier well appointed, in a good capacity and condition to dispute it out with any of his adversaries.

Conclusion 2:

Every true believer has a constant fighting work before God, and there is no end of his war in this world, not any time in which he can stop fighting. It is not so with other soldiers. There is a time when kings go to battle (2 Sam. 1:1ff), and there is a time when they disband their ranks, or draw them into their winter quarters, or make a cessation of all hostility by leagues or truces. There is a time of war (the Preacher says, Eccl. 3:8) and a time of peace. Other soldiers are not always fighting. But a Christian's duty and employment is to fight continually. He cannot assure himself of any respite or intermission in the course of his warfare. This may be convincingly made out in three or four particulars.

1. Every believer reaches after, marching towards the perfect enjoyment of the blessed fruits of the everlasting love of God in Christ. This is the prize he runs for, the crown he looks for, the recompence of reward he has respect unto, the end and aim of his race and wrestling. He is in his journey or on his march towards that city which has foundations made by God (Heb. 11:10). It is in that better country, where he may enjoy the glorious fruits of the peculiar love of God in perfection. Every Christian is in a wayfaring state, and declares plainly (by the course he shapes and steers) that he is a stranger here, and seeking a country, (Heb. 11:14), travelling towards the heavenly Canaan, and the face of his soul is set towards that Jerusalem which is above. He has grace and glory in his eye, and is engaged

in a close and eager pursuit of happiness. The end of his faith and holy conversation is the salvation of his soul, and the perfect and perpetual fruition of the love of God in the brightest discoveries and richest effusions of it.

    2. Every believer meets with great opposition in his march and way to this God, from enemies that try to make headway against him, and do what they can to separate him from the love of God in Christ Jesus. He meets with numerous adversaries that design and drive at this to hinder himself and the rest of Gods people in their travels to Canaan, to divert and turn them out of the road of holiness and obedience, which leads to happiness. They attempt to pluck them (if it were possible) out of God's hand, to tear them out of his loving embraces, to cut them short of the blessed fruition of the love of God in Christ. God leads every believer, as it were, through the land of the Philistines where they must see war, and brings him to the heavenly Canaan that way. And he meets with this opposition in a few *ways:*

    1). From himself, and that sin that dwells in him. From his own heart and nature, as it is depraved and vitiated. From his natural corruption, or that sin that is inlaid and connected in his nature. This is the principal, the capital, the grand enemy, that is bred in his bowels, raising intestine civil wars, without which his foreign enemies, the rest of his adversaries could not hurt him, nor make any considerable head against him. It was the great advantage of the Captain of our salvation, (as our

Savior is called in Heb. 2:10), in all his engagements with Satan and his instruments, that he was holy, harmless, undefiled, and separate from sinners, (Heb. 7:26). That he did not know any sin, (2 Cor. 5:21). That he had no sin in him. Here, it was that just before his last and greatest encounter with Satan, he tells his disciples, "the prince of this world cometh and hath nothing in me," (John 14:30). There was nothing in our Lord Jesus that complied with, or was suitable to the temptations of the God of this world. Nothing to close with his suggestions, or entertain his terrors. The enemy without had no correspondents within him, Satan could not lay hands, or fasten a temptation on him. Christ threw him off with ease in this respect. Here he was tempted indeed in all points, like as we are, yet without sin, (Heb. 4:15). Temptation to Christ was like throwing a piece of dry paper on mirror; it will not stick. The sin of our natures is Satan's strength and advantage. He finds enough in the best of believers, that found nothing in our Savior. Satan's sparks easily consume us, because he finds so much tinder in us. The lusts within us are ready to take fire at every injection. There is a traitor in our own bowels that is ready to open our ports, and let in the adversary.

Now of the war which a Christian wages with this home-bred, intestine enemy, the seventh chapter of this epistle to the Romans gives us a clear account. Where the apostle raises an out-cry, and makes doleful complaints of the remainders of sin, the law in the members, the body of sin and death, and discourses of the nature, power and prevalence of indwelling sin, as to some engagements. The apostle James speaks of the lusts that war in our members, (James 4:1). And Peter speaks of fleshly lusts that war against the soul, (1 Peter 2:11). These make up that opposite party within a Christian that would intercept and stop him in his way to glory: a secret, subtle, treacherous, designing party that creates him a world of trouble and danger in his journey towards heaven.

2). From the world, which is another enemy that would obviate and intercept the people of God in their travels. Here the world was a part of Christ's glorious conquest. "Be of good cheer, I have overcome the world," (John 16:33). And the believer that is born of God by faith in the Lord Jesus Christ overcomes it too, (1 John 5:4), which plainly implies that the world is an enemy. Considerable are the expressions of the apostle to this purpose, James 4:4, "Know ye not that the friendship of the world is enmity with God? Whosoever therefore will be a friend of the world, is the enemy of God." And does it not follow from here, that he that is a friend of God is an enemy to the world, as it lies in opposition to God, and the world (in that respect) an enemy to him? The world is one of the associates of that false party within a Christian, and under the conduct of Satan militates against a believer. Particularly:

1]. The snares and allurements of the world, which would carry away and seduce a Christian from following after God. These make war on a child of God; and are dangerous enemies. As they say, *fight with silver or gold weapons, and never doubt of victory.* Some enemies have bought great victories, which they could never have won otherwise. All these things will give you profit, pleasure, and honor, (the flattering world says to a believer) *if you will fall down, or surrender to me.* These ensnaring and alluring objects, which the world presents the sons of men with, have such a close and intimate correspondence with the lusts in their hearts, and what is carnal in them, that they fight against their souls with great advantage and success. The apostle having moved on from the love of the world, and the things that are in the world, sums up all that is in the world in those three particulars, the lust of the flesh, the lust of the eyes, and the pride of life, (1 John 2:4-5). The apostle speaks as if there were nothing else in the world but lusting, because there is such a curse which has come on all creature-enjoyments with reference to man, that so far as he is of the world, they are objects of lust to him. They are things that are exciting, drawing forth, invigorating and improving that lust and corruption that is in him. By these lusts the apostle means the several respective objects, and puts the lust which is in us for the things themselves lusted after, carnal pleasures, profits and preferments. He does not say sensual pleasures, riches, and honor (though he speaks of them), but the *lusts of the flesh and eye*, and *pride of life*. This is because our lusts render them evil to us (how lawful they might be in themselves as objects are) and make them objects of temptation and seduction from the Lord, putting a painted whorish beauty and tempting luster on them, varnishing them, and making false representations of them. Yes, it is evident (as the good Dr. Owen observes in his *Treatise of Temptation*.[5]

> That all these things (the lust of the flesh, *etc.*) are principally in the subject, not in the object; in the heart not in the world. But they are said to be in the world, because the world gets into them, mixes itself with them, unites, and incorporates them. As faith and the promises are said to be mixed, (Heb. 4:2), so are lust and temptation (from worldly objects) mixed; they twist together, a mutual improvement one from another, grow each of them higher and higher by the mutual strength they administer to one another.

From this mixture, union, and incorporation of the objects in the world with the lusts in the hearts of men, and their firm and close combination together, it comes to pass that the enticing, tempting world is a very potent and prevailing adversary to the souls of men. And that believers themselves in whom the lusts mentioned are but *in part* mortified and subdued) have hard work sometimes to stand their ground against the snares and

---

[5] Page 68.

allurements and bewitching insinuations of a deceitful world. To this point, reduce sinful examples in the world, counsels of carnal friends, the friendship of the world, which is enmity to God and good men, (James 4:4), and false doctrines which are spots out of the world (1 John 4:5). These are calculated to the corrupt desires, inclinations and interests of the men of the world, and therefore, of a very great resentment with them. In a word, all worldly lusts (as the apostle calls them, Titus 2:12) that are so many baits and snares to entangle and entice the people of God to desert the holy and good ways of the Lord. Those golden sins that are thrown down before a Christian to invite him to gaze on them, and stoop to take them up, so that he may be retarded and stopped in his course, and lose the prize he runs for.

2]. The troubles and frightful afflictions of the world. This concerns the formidable, frightful afflictions and persecutions that would impede or retard and hinder the people of God in their travels towards that heavenly country, where the sweet fruits of divine love are to be enjoyed in the greatest maturity and perfection of them. This is the *tribulation in the world* against which the Lord Jesus lays down in great encouragement from the consideration of his own conquest of the world, (John 16:33). Of this ill will and entertainment in the world, the afflictions that the children of God must expect to contest with, the apostle discourses in Romans 8:35-37, where he mentions tribulation, distress, persecution, famine, nakedness, peril, sword, and such like formidable things to nature, oppose the faithful in their way, and make war on them. A Christian lies open to many sharp and fiery trials, (1 Peter 4:12). And must look to endure a great fight or contention of afflictions, (Heb. 10:32). The world can put on two faces, and change its countenance as occasion serves. If pretended flattering smiles will not do, then killing frowns shall, if it is possible. The world has terrors to frighten them with, as well as allurements to entice believers out of the way of happiness. The men of the world are usually barbs in the eyes, and thorns or scourges in the sides of believers. Briers and thorns are with them in the world (as the Lord tells the prophet in Ezek. 2:6) that will scratch the face of their reputation, wound them in their outward concernments, and tear their flesh. Yes, they dwell among scorpions, that will put them to great torment, and sting them to death. A fellow named Aelian made reports concerning the Lybians, *ocreatos dormire solera,* that they were accustomed to sleep with their boots on, lest the scorpions, their country was infested with, should sting them. I am sure a Christian has need to walk around with boots, and have his feet shod with the preparation of the gospel of peace. Yes, he is to be defended and prepared in all respects, or he will be in much danger of that which is worse than scorpions in this way.[6] As believers have bodies of flesh and mortality, that keep open a house for sicknesses, pains, diseases, and give

---

[6] See Mr. Greenhill on Ezek. 2:6.

entertainment to them, so they are exposed to the rage and power of unreasonable men. They pass through an enemy country, where they have many affronts and indignities offered to them. If lies and calumnies, scoffs and scorns, angry looks and cruel threatenings, opprobrious and injurious dealings, or any kind of cruelty may be likely to scare a believer out of his way, or force him to a dishonorable retreat, or to run from his colors by quitting his profession. In this the malignant angry world will be sure (if the Lord permits) to prove him in that way. In both the respects mentioned, the world is an enemy, and makes opposition to believers in their way to glory. Furthermore, a believer meets with *opposition:*

3]. From Satan, the prince and god of the world, (Eph. 6:11-12). If a Christian were to put a trial to his masteries, and make a contest only with flesh and blood (whether we understand by this his own corruptions, or opposition from men, like himself) he would have hot and hard service in it. But this is his case and lot, to meet with opposition from principalities and powers, the rulers of the darkness of this world, and spiritual wickedness in high places. He fights at great disadvantage with enemies, that hold the hill and upper-ground. He combats hand to hand with the god of this world; as well as his creatures, the men of the world. Satan is one of the allies of indwelling sin, and of confederacy with our own hearts, which are ready every moment, if there is not a strict watch kept on them, to betray us into his hands, and deliver us up to him. A Christian has need to look to himself, considering that Satan goes about daily seeking to devour, (1 Peter 5:8). A believer will be sure to meet with this lion in his way. And our flesh and hearts (as was intimated before) are Satan's correspondents and confederates against the spiritual life, and comfort, and happiness of our souls, ready to open up to him, make a surrender of all, and agree with him in all his dangerous and destructive applications of himself to us. This spiritual leviathan is a crooked serpent, (Isa. 27:1). Sometimes, he opposes the people of God by force, and then he is a piercing serpent, sometimes he circumvents them by craft, and then he is a crooked serpent. *Vel rectus venit, vel tortuosus.* Satan opposes the people of God in a way of fraud, (he plays the dragon and deceives them. He is a serpent; yes, an old serpent, (Rev. 12:9). He has his wiles, (Eph. 6:11). He has his advantageous devices, (2 Cor. 2:11). He has his methods of deceit, and his depths or deep contrivances, (Rev 2:24). And in a way of force and violence, he acts the part of a lion and rages. He has his venomous arrows, his fiery darts, (Eph. 6:16), and makes many violent onsets on the children of God. The church of God, or the body of saints and called ones in the world, have the gates of hell (Matt. 16:18), that is (as it is commonly expounded) the power and policy of the devil, and his instruments, and under-agents, to oppose them in their way to heaven, though they shall not prevail in that opposition. *Lastly:*

4]. From death itself, which is the last enemy, (1 Cor. 15:26). When all the rest are beaten out of the field, and a Christian is marching off and ready to make his triumphant entrance into heaven, death encounters him. This comes in by the curse. And its natural or direct tendency is to separate a son of Adam from God forever. It is the great and grand executioner of the vindictive justice of God. Here men enjoy some fruits of (at least) the general and common goodness of God. But when death comes, it pushes them away from God, makes an everlasting separation between them, and all the fruits of the goodness of God, turns them into hell, where they must feed on the bitter fruit of their own ways forever. When death has done its execution on the condemned sons and daughters of Adam, God will then carry away all his goodness from them, and never afford them so much as one drop of water to cool their tongues to eternity.

That which makes death so terrible is, that in the ordinary course of it, it makes a perfect and perpetual separation between the sons and daughters of men, and all the fruits of the love, and goodness, and patience of the blessed God. "Death passed upon all men," for that all have sinned, (Rom. 5:12). And where it reigns and triumphs, and is victorious over any man, and fastens its sting in him (as I may allude to 1 Cor. 15:55), it destroys him utterly by putting him into a condition of everlasting separation from God. Now, this is the last adversary that the believing Christian soldier contends with; though on more advantageous terms then other men.

So much for the second particular under the second conclusion. Every believer meets with great opposition in his way.

3. A believer cannot possibly make his way through all these enemies, and cannot come down against all this opposition without fighting. He skirmishes with these enemies, yes, fights many high battles against them. He must put on the whole armor of God, Eph. 6:11), and keep it on, and make use of the weapons of his Christian warfare, and his faith and other graces will be soundly put to it. It costs him many a bickering. He runs, and wrestles, and labors, and strives, and fights the good fight of faith, as we might demonstrate by many scripture instances. He does this by fighting, I mean a vigorous contending and conflicting with the enemies of his soul, which is expressed variously by the Holy Spirit in scripture. He must strive hard that will enter in at the strait gate, (Luke 13:24). Ordinary seeking will not do it. If the believer takes off his armor, lays down his weapons, suffers the sword of faith to rust in the scabbard, and does not draw it forth as there is occasion; if he hangs down his hands in prayer, sinks in his hopes, cools in his courage, and stands still in a secure careless manner, it will be impossible that he should break through those legions of devils, those armies of temptations, and make

his way through those adverse powers, that oppose themselves in his way to happiness.

 4. As the opposition from, at least, some of his enemies is perpetual in this life, so the believer has no rest, but has work enough every day to contest with them. A believer has a restless enemy to contend with, as Hannibal said of Marcellus the Roman consul, *let him conquer or be conquered*, for he would never be quiet nor give over, neither give rest to his enemy, nor take rest himself, otherwise he would be at it still, and never have done anything. So, may we say much more of the believer's enemies. Satan never draws his forces out of the field. Corruptions one way or other will be stirring, and the Christian shall be exercised in it with some thorn in the flesh, and buffetings of Satan's messenger. The people in Nehemiah's time, when they were alarmed and afraid of their malicious and malignant neighbors, worked with one hand and held a weapon in the other, (Neh. 4:17). But such is the case of a Christian, that he must not only work, with a weapon in the other hand, but he must actually use his weapon while he is working. He is to be fighting with one hand, and building or laboring with the other. If his enemies conquer, they will be sure to prosecute their victory to the utmost, and lose no advantage. If they are overtaken and routed in any particular engagement, they will not fail to rally their forces, recruit and reinforce themselves presently and fall on again. So that a Christian has need to eat and drink and sleep while he is *at arms*. He has no

time to put off his armor, to lay down his weapons. He will be hotly engaged until (Acts 3:19), the times of refreshing and cooling shall come. He can never be said in this world to be discharged from his wars. If a Christian lives to seventy years of age or more, he is not by such an age, retired, nor can he plead age or anything else to excuse himself from the duty of a soldier. Verily there is no discharge in this warfare on this side of the grave. There is no bringing of these enemies to a composition, no cessation to be made, no league or truce to be admitted in this warfare. A Christian must be constantly fighting and contending against the enemies of his peace and happiness. So much for the second conclusion.

Conclusion 3:

A true believer is never totally and absolutely conquered in any engagement with the enemies that war against him. To be conquered by sin (the sense I take it here) is to be separated from the love of God, and utterly deprived of its special fruits. "Who shall separate us" (the apostle says in Romans 8:35) "from the love of Christ?" That is, who shall conquer us? "I am persuaded that neither death nor life, nor angel," *etc.* "shall be able to separate us from the love of God, which is in Christ Jesus our Lord," (Rom. 8:38-39). What Paul means is that a Christian can never be *totally* conquered, notwithstanding all the opposition that is made against him. Let enemies do what they can against him, yet if he is not separated from the love of God, he is not absolutely conquered, or defeated of his happiness. In this respect a believer is never conquered. *For:*

1. Nothing befalls him in his warfare, notwithstanding what his enemies attempt against him, that turns away the heart of God utterly from him. Though sin and Satan may prevail *very far* in some conflicts, yet never to such a degree as to provoke the Lord to reject him, and cast him out of his favor. God may be provoked by the compliances of a believer at some turns with sin and Satan and the world to take away the manifestations of his love, to deny him some expressions of his favor, to visit his transgressions with a rod, and his iniquity with stripes, but never to take his lovingkindness utterly from him, (Psalm 89:30–33). A believer may be so foiled and overcome by his enemies, through the neglect of his watch, or otherwise, that God may be displeased with him, that there may be a discontinuance of the sensible expressions of the love of God to him, and an interruption of it as to manifestations: and yet there is no intermission of the love of God to him, as to *its being*. His love to him is unchangeable and everlasting.

2. Nothing falls out in his progress or march that absolutely diverts him from his course of proceeding, or moving towards the enjoyment of the sweet fruits of divine love. A believer may be wounded, battered, and pressed down, but not totally checked in his way, and

turned aside from it. He may receive many a blow that staggers him, that makes him reel and complain, that wounds him in his graces and comforts. David had his bones broken, received deep and dangerous wounds that were long healing, that sank him and were corrupt, (Psalm 38:5, 7-8), because he did not apply a timely remedy to them; they were not presently searched and looked after. He was knocked down and lay in a swoon for a great while, that those about him might be ready to fear he would never come to himself again. But he revived and recovered at last. Satan prevailed with him to commit folly with Bathsheba, to murder and imbrue his hands in the blood of Uriah, to vent his pride and vain glorious state in the numbering of the people, and to incur the displeasure of God by these things. But all this did not expel the love of God out of his heart, or divert him totally from prosecuting its enjoyment. Take a believer in his lowest condition, when he is most overwhelmed and prevailed on by his enemies, yet, at that time, there is the seed of God remaining in him (1 John 3:9). That inclines and carries him Godward. There is a power of grace, and a work of the Spirit on his heart that gives him an inclination, bent, and tendency Godward continually. And though temptations may turn him out of the way for a time, and he may meet with many rubs and impediments in his Christian race, yet there is the strong bias of grace, the poise and impression of God's Spirit on his heart that inclines and carries him Godward. In this he will come in again, though he may be turned off for a while. That general bent and inclination of his heart towards God, as his last end and greatest good, and towards his commandments, as the only best rules of living and walking, is ever preserved in the believer by the mighty power of God (according to his covenant-engagement) even then when his enemies have gotten him down and laid him at their feet. So that if the Lord never takes away his loving-kindness utterly from the believer, nor the believer totally lose his love to God, then what follows? But that there can be no separation of a true believer from the love of God in Christ Jesus, and by consequence that he cannot be absolutely conquered in anything, though he may be overcome in some engagements.

Conclusion 4:

Every true believer manages a successful war, and is sure of a conquest. My meaning is not that every Christian has a certainty of persuasion that he shall prevail, or overcome; for many are ready to say sometimes that he shall one day fall by the hand of this or that *Saul*. But there is a certainty of the thing in itself. I speak of the certainty of the object, or the truth of this proposition, that every believer shall certainly conquer the enemies of his soul, not of the certainty of the subject, but the certainty and assurance that he shall be victorious at last, and in the end. A believer shall certainly win the day and conquer all opposers, whatever his unbelieving heart may at any time suggest to the contrary. Here Paul speaks of it as a thing *done*. "We do more than overcome." This may be understood in the following manner:

1. A believer in this life gets many indicating victories. He is not able indeed utterly to drive out the Canaanites, they will abide in his land (I mean in his heart) and be rebelling and vexing him frequently. But the Lord gives him many remarkable victories over them. There are some memorable days and happy times in which the people of God come out of the field victorious, and triumph over their spiritual enemies. They set their feet in the neck of their lusts, and lay their corruptions bleeding at their feet, and do so resist Satan as to route him and put him to flight.

2. If he is for a time overcome, yet he recovers himself at last and overcomes the day. He may be overcome, and carried captive (as the apostle intimates in Romans 7:23). He may be remarkably overcome in some particular conflicts, and taken prisoner. But he cannot be detained always a prisoner, all the power and policy of his adversaries cannot hold him. He will make an escape from them sooner or later, and obtain rescue and deliverance. If he is foiled, and laid on his back for a time; yet it is not long before he recovers himself, and gets up again by godly sorrow, humiliation and repentance, and renews the combat, and is too hard for his enemies. If he is routed, he rallies again, and never

leaves fighting, until he carries the day, and goes out of the field as a conqueror.

    3. His enemies lose ground by all their partial conquests of him. A child of God gets good by his foils and falls, yes, gets ground insensibly of his corruptions and other enemies by it. His enemies by winning the day, lose it; and by conquering, are conquered. Every victory that sin and Satan obtain, makes a gracious heart more humble, more sensible of his own weakness, and absolute need of the strength of Christ, more watchful against sin and temptation, more cautious for time to come of admitting parleys and compliances with his adversaries, and so turns (through the over-ruling hand of grace) to the singular advantage of a Christian in many respects. Lay these things together, and it will be manifest that a believer manages a very successful war, and is sure at last of an absolute conquest.

Conclusion 5:

    A believer's victory and conquest are incomparably glorious. His conquest is most exceedingly glorious. There Paul says, "we are more than conquerors." We do not *only* conquer, but triumph; we have a triumphant victory. We are much too hard for our enemies, we do more than overcome, we *do* over-overcome. Grotius says that Paul loves the composition of words with the prepositions he uses, and he gives many other instances (besides this in the text) of such compositions in Paul's epistles of this emphasis. When he speaks of the *rich* grace of God, or of the *great and glorious* privileges of his children, he thinks he cannot over state these things. They are such things, that, as Luther said of God and heaven, do not admit, are not capable of a hyperbole. No expression is so high, or superlative, as to transcend and exceed the measure of the excellency of such things.

Now the greatness and gloriousness of a believer's victory appears in many things, which we shall but glance at, as we pass along. Glorious it is, in that the believer conquers in suffering, when he is in appearance conquered, overcome and destroyed. When he is slain with the sword, devoured by lions, burnt to ashes attached to a stake, sawn asunder, or any way violently put to death; yet in all these things *he conquers*, as the martyrs have done. They overcome by the blood of the Lamb, the word of their testimony, and not loving their lives to the death. Gualther takes this to be the sense of the apostle. "In all these things we are more than conquerors." He does not say we overcome all these things, so as that they shall be no more, or cease to oppose us; but in all these things we conquer. For afflictions remain, and will remain as long as the world lasts, nor will persecutions ever cease, which beget banishment, famine, nakedness and the sword to the godly. But in these things, and among all these perils and evils of suffering, the faithful *more* than overcome. And this is admirable that they overcome even when they are slain, or burned, or destroyed any other-way.

They are killed all the day long, accounted (and used) as sheep for the slaughter; as in the verse before the text, and yet they are more than conquerors. Human, carnal reason cannot comprehend this. It is indeed mysterious and glorious. Again, it is glorious in that he conquers such enemies as conquer all but himself, and such as he is. The great conquerors of the world have been slaves to their own pride, ambition, vain-glory, covetousness, and other base lusts, which a Christian subdues and conquers. Many of them have been Satan's slaves, when they have been masters of the world. But the believer resists the devil, and puts him to flight. He overcomes himself (which is a nobler exploit then to overcome and conquer nations) sets his foot on Satan, tramples and crushes that serpent, (Romans 16:20). He treads the world under his feet, as the church of God. The woman mentioned in Rev. 12:1 is said to have the moon (that is, all these changeable earthly things) under her feet. No, he overcomes death itself, which tramples on and prevails over other conquerors. Death stings, kills, and ruins other men, but cannot hurt a Christian, because it cannot separate him from God. "Oh death! Where is thy sting? Oh grave, where is thy victory?" (1 Cor. 15:55). Those words which are commonly translated "the gates of hell," (Matt. 16:18), and are thought to import the power and policy of the devil, are rendered by learned Cameron, "the gates of the grave," or death, alleging that the word for it never but once in scripture signifies hell, but either the grave, or the state and condition of a deceased person. And he conceives the mind of our Savior in that expression to be, that though the faithful lie dead for a time as well as other men, death exercises a dominion over them, the worm feeds sweetly on them, they are imprisoned in the grave, and lie bound hand and foot with the cords of death (Psalm 18:3). Yet that the power of death and the grave shall not finally prevail over them. The abolition of the destructive dominion of death is intended by the Lord Jesus, according to this exposition. Cyprian says "Christians may die, but cannot be overcome. Death may kill them, but cannot conquer them." The victory of believers over their enemies is very glorious in this respect. It is also glorious in that a believer conquers his enemies by conquering himself, crucifying himself (the flesh with the affections and lusts, Gal 5:24). He does it by subduing his own spirit, beating down his own body and bringing it into subjection (1 Cor. 9:27). He does it by plucking out an offending right eye, cutting off an offending right hand, (Matt. 5:29-30). This is a strange execution on himself in the path of mortification, which is both a noble and a strange way *of conquering*. He overcomes *himself* and by this overcomes all his enemies.

    Moreover, it is glorious in that he is so far from being separated from the love of God by the opposition which his enemies make against him, that he is by it greatly furthered in the way to the perfect enjoyment of its fruits. His enemies, whether they will or not, help him to a most glorious conquest. For all things (how adverse and opposite no matter what they are) work for his good, (Romans 8:28). That is, for his most glorious, everlasting triumph in the highest heavens. As the afflictions and troubles which happened to Paul in the course of his ministerial warfare fell out to the furtherance of the gospel, (Phil. 1:12). So, the opposition which a believer meets with from all his adversaries, falls out to the furtherance of his victorious proceedings in the course of his Christian warfare, and of his after-triumph and glory. No, this victory is glorious, in that he gives his enemies a total defeat and overthrow at last. He has a perfect and absolute victory and conquest over them, so as never to be molested with them anymore. He passes to heaven through the midst of his enemies, and gets out of the reach of their opposition, or molestation, and there triumphs gloriously to eternity.

Conclusion 6:

Every believer obtains this glorious victory and conquest through the Lord Jesus Christ. "We are more than conquerors through him that loved us," that is, through Jesus Christ, or God in Christ which is the same thing. The apostle having discoursed excellently of this spiritual war with one of the greatest enemies that a Christian has to do with, namely, in-dwelling sin, issues all triumphantly in thanks to God through Christ for deliverance and victory, (Rom. 7). And having spoken of death and the grave, very formidable adversaries, and triumphed over them, thanks God who gives victory through Christ, (1 Cor. 15:55-57). And there is the same reason as to all the enemies of a Christian. A believer obtains this incomparable victory and glorious conquest over all through Christ. *For:*

    1. The Lord Jesus Christ has procured and purchased this victory and conquest for believers. Therefore, he has suffered and died, satisfied and merited, that his people might obtain a glorious victory over sin, Satan, the world, death, and all their enemies. The foundation of this victory has been laid by a high hand of grace in the death and mediation of the Lord Jesus. Man having revolted from under the government and dominion of God's revealed will and law, and thrown off his obedience, made an election of sin and Satan for his lords and sovereigns; the holy God in justice and righteous severity, delivers him up to the authority and sovereignty of sin and Satan, and his spiritual enemies, even death itself. And they put in their claim to a sovereignty, yes, and actually exercise a dominion over him; so that man in this condition is a captive, prisoner, slave, and cannot get his liberty. If he struggles sometimes, and rises up to war against them, all his contendings are vain, he is overcome presently, and held in bondage. The reason is, because his enemies are (in a sense) as strong as the law and justice of God. The strength of sin (and by parity of reason, of other

enemies) is the law, (1 Cor. 15:56). That is, the law broken, and the justice of God offended. But the Lord Jesus having satisfied and merited, when there is an application of that redemption which is in Christ to any man; now sin, Satan, and the world have no right to exercise this dominion; they lose their claim and title to such dominion, and this is the foundation of any man's conquest of them. Here though sin may tyrannize sometimes, yet it shall not reign over them; not have any of their enemies any right to conquer or prevail, as before. No, Christ has paid the great price, and bought the victory for them of him in whose hand it is to adjudge it to them. They overcome by the blood of the Lamb, (Rev. 12:11).

2. He has actually in his own person conquered their enemies for them, "be of good comfort (our Savior says) I have overcome the world," (John 16:33). That is, the lusts of the world, the men of the world, the prince of the world, the shares, temptations, terrors and evils of the world. He has bruised the serpent's head, (Gen. 3:15). Destroyed the works of the devil, (1 John 3:8). Now (the Lord Jesus says with reference to the time of his sufferings) is the judgement of this world, now shall the prince of this world be cast out, (John 12:31). The dethroning of Satan, and destruction of his dominion by Jesus Christ is that which is intended in that expression. Here the apostle says, that he "spoiled principalities and powers," and made a "shew of them openly triumphing over them in it" (that is, his cross) or in himself, (Col.

2:15). The Lord Jesus took away the prey or booty of souls, which Satan had gotten, and led away the devil and his angels, as prisoners of war. He stripped principalities and powers, that is, the apostate angels, of all their titles they had gotten by the world by the sin of man, yes, he triumphed over them as captives to be disposed of at his pleasure. He has bound the strong man armed and spoiled his goods. In this way Christ is said to wound the head (for so is it in the original, not heads) but over many countries, (Psalm 110:6), by the head, the large earth. Some understand Satan that rules as head over the children of disobedience everywhere. I judge it better to propound it to the most comprehensive sense, and then the meaning is, that Christ breaks in pieces the head, that is, the counsel and power of Satan and all his instruments, crushing and conquering all the enemies of his people. He has conquered death itself, and having grappled and fought with that serpent, he has pulled out the sting, and he has disarmed that king of terrors, that he may be in no condition to hurt and ruin his people. Death can be no longer a curse to them; but a blessing, an outlet as to misery and an in-let to all happiness. He has conquered and triumphed over all the enemies of believers, virtually on his cross, but actually and effectually in his exaltation. He did this when he "ascended up on high, he led captivity captive," (Eph. 4:8; Psalm 68:18). And he has conquered and triumphed over all our enemies, not for himself, but on our behalf, and for our advantage. Hieron said, "The victory of the

Lord is the triumph of the servants." Well may the army of believers be assured of victory and triumph, when as they fight with a conquered enemy, and their general alone in his own person has routed their adversaries.

  3. He puts them into a conquering-capacity. He sends his spirit to make the application of his redemption to all his redeemed ones by working faith in their hearts, drawing them to himself, giving them an actual interest in himself, and his benefits, and putting them into a state of justification, which is a state of victory and triumph. A justified person is in a conquering-capacity and condition. He is under grace, and not under the law, therefore, neither sin, nor any other enemy shall have dominion over him, (Rom. 6:14). Take an elect person, that was given to Christ by the Father from eternity, and redeemed by Christ in the fulness of time, yet before his effectual vocation, he is under the feet of his enemies, in no better condition to fight it out with them then other men; sin, and Satan, and the world are much too hard for him. But when once the Spirit of Christ has worked an effectual work of grace in his soul, and by uniting him to the Lord Jesus has brought him into a state of justification, now he is in a condition to dispute it out to the last with all his enemies, and to win the day as well. A justified person is invincible, he cannot be conquered; and he is victorious, none of his enemies can stand before him. Victory and triumph are adjudged by the Lord to a state of justification, and are infallible consequences of it. Here

we find Paul's comfortable persuasion, and triumphant expressions in Rom. 8:38-39. Now all the people of God are admitted into this state of justification, and in its glorious privileges, through the Lord Jesus Christ.

4. He furnishes believers with skill, and strength, and courage, and weapons, and all war-like furniture, and military qualifications, and accomplishments. They are in all respects well-appointed for the war. It is the Lord Jesus that sets them forth and furnishes them with all his weapons for the battle. The Lord Jesus Christ is the Christians magazine. All those armor and weapons which a believer uses in his spiritual conflicts (of which you have an enumeration in Eph. 6:6, 13-14, *etc.*) Are such as come out of Christ's armory. As he puts the believer into a conquering state, in his justification, so he gives him conquering abilities in his sanctification. He gives them skill and valor, and resolution, and all other qualifications and endowments that a militant condition calls for.

5. He administers seasonable supplies and recruits of grace and strength to them. He sends them auxiliary forces and gives them such assistance as they need for every conflict. He gives power to them when they are faint, and when they have no might, increases their strength, (Isa. 40:29). He gives them a sufficiency of grace, and his power rests on them. Here when they are weak, yet then they are strong, (2 Cor. 12:9-10). Because habitual inherent grace will not carry them through their difficult engagements, therefore he affords

actual, and occasional assistance as their necessities require. This is all that seasonable help which is administered to believers from the throne of grace (Heb. 4:16). It comes from the Lord Jesus Christ. They have the immutable assistance of the Spirit of Christ that dwells in them. They must necessarily overcome in this respect, because greater it is that is in them, then he that is in the world, (1 John 4:4). Here the apostle, that had low thoughts of himself, and was as much nothing in his own eyes as any man, yet attributes a kind of omnipotence to himself. "I can do all things through Christ which strengtheneth me," (Phil. 4:13). He strengthens them with all might, (Col. 1:11).

Conclusion 7:

The love of God in Christ is the absolute first cause of those victorious proceedings, and this infallible conquest of believers. *For:*

1. The everlasting love of God determines, that the victory shall fall on the side of believers. The will of God is that all believers shall conquer. Here the apostle lays the foundation of this triumph in divine predestination, and in God's being "for us," (Rom. 8:30-31). Those that are appointed to obtain salvation by Jesus Christ (as it may be concluded of all believers; living faith being a special fruit of election) may meet with many enemies in their way, but shall infallibly

break through all opposition, and get to heaven at last. The love of God has decreed them victory.

2. The everlasting love of God lays in suitable provision of means for an infallible conquest. Divine love concluded on the mission of Christ into the world, to purchase it for his people, and obtain the victory in his own person, as a common person representing all believers. This love gives them a General (the Lord Jesus Christ) that is invincible, the captain of the host of the Lord, that appeared to Joshua, (Joshua 5:13-14). It arms them with invincible graces, offensive and defensive; and orders them the insuperable and invincible assistance of the Spirit of Christ, and the needful supplies and recruits of assisting grace. The love of God in Christ furnishes the Christian soldier completely in every way with all that he needs in order to conquer his enemies. In this he is better provided for in the combat, and has more assistance in the combat, and more assurance (consequently) of success, then any other conquerors have. The Christian soldier is well appointed and set forth for the war, recruited and assisted in it at the cost and charges of the love of God in Jesus Christ.

3. The everlasting love of God adjudges them triumph at last and crowns them with it. Divine love sets the glorious crown on the head of the persevering, victorious, all-conquering believer. There is a glorious day coming, in which the believer shall receive the reward of all his labors and travails and combats with the flesh, the world, and the devil. And this reward will

be adjudged to him that overcomes, and actually conferred on him by the grace and love of God in Jesus Christ. Not his merit, but God's mercy and love will then crown him. His present sufferings in the time of his warfare are not worthy to be compared with the glory that shall be revealed in him, (Rom. 8:18). When Paul had fought his good fight, and finished the course of his warfare, he expected his triumphant crown from the Lord, the righteous Judge, (2 Tim. 4:7-8), which is a crown of mercy and grace, and also a crown of righteousness. In it is the sweet concurrence of the remunerative justice of God with his infinite mercy, grace, and love in that glorious work of crowning a persevering Christian soldier with everlasting triumph and glory. Divine love adjudges and bestows on believers at last the heavenly prize they run for, and the incorruptible crown they fight for in this world. That they triumph eternally is from the love of God in Christ. So much for the doctrinal part.

Chapter 3:
Uses of the Doctrine

Use 1.

We might improve this observation, to crush that erroneous conceit of the Arminians, concerning the possibility of a regenerate man's total and final apostacy. For to assert this, is to say, that a believer may be totally defeated and overcome, and sin, Satan and the world may prevail over him to his utter ruin. The truth we have explained, is ready pressed to militate against the men of that heretical persuasion. And it is alone (without the levy of any other forces) of sufficient strength to fight that enemy and beat him out of the field. This text of the apostle, and the observation we have deduced from it, strikes those adversaries of the doctrine of perseverance under the fifth rib, or rather stabs their fifth article concerning the apostacy of saints to the heart. This one weapon, if it is well managed and wielded, will do a real and thorough execution. For if there may be a total and final defection of believers, or falling from grace, and out of the favor of God, then there is a possibility that a believer may be totally and finally separated from the love of God, and so, totally conquered; which is diametrically opposite to the strain and genius, and intent of the apostle's discourse and what we have been regularly building on it. But let it be enough to have in this way faced that grand enemy the Arminian, without engaging further on this occasion in any pitched confutation of him.

Use 2.

This makes it appear who are the bravest soldiers, the most renowned warriors, people of the greatest bravery and gallantry in the world. They are believing men and women. A Christian man or woman is by many degrees a better soldier then Caesar or Alexander. Sincere believers, of all degrees and conditions, are people of eminency this way. Among the victorious worthies, whose famous exploits and achievements are recorded, (Hebrews 11), the apostle does not leave believing women out of the catalogue. We read of great exploits that have been performed, even by those of the weaker sex, both in sacred and common history. But none are to be compared with those which believing women, through faith, have enterprised and accomplished. "O woman, great is thy faith," our Savior says in Matthew 15:28. Why then it might be said also, O woman, great is thy victory! For this is the victory that overcomes the world, even our faith, (1 John 5:4). True faith, though it is but as a grain of a mustard seed, will overcome and bear down all that opposition the world can make against it. As to this Christian warfare, victory and triumph, believers of all sorts share in it. There is no difference in this matter, but Jew and Greek, bond and free, male and female are all one in this respect through Jesus Christ. The weakest believer will be too hard for the strongest adversary. This is a clear consequence from what we have discoursed, that a believer is the bravest, and most victorious soldier in the world.

Use 3.

A word of singular encouragement and comfort to all that mourn for the sorrowful state and condition of Jerusalem. Know it, and believe it, that the church of God, however afflicted and oppressed in the world, shall certainly prevail and overcome in the day at last. The victories and triumphs that God has decreed and determined shall certainly be awarded and given to the conflicting militant-church in its season. How might we expostulate the case with the mightiest of the church's adversaries? With the high and low, great and small ones of the earth in this respect? *Why do the nations rage and people imagine a vain thing?* It is vain, and will be found so in the issue, to oppose the Lord Jesus, to fight against his members, to plot, design and endeavor the ruin of the interest of Christ in the way for the Lord Jesus, and his called, and faithful and chosen, shall certainly be more then overcome at last. The Lamb and his followers shall be victorious and illustrious conquerors. The beast may arise out of the bottomless pit, and raise the army of hell, come with legions of vile devils, and their instruments, and set their hellish armies in array, and make war on the witnesses and overcome them for a while. But they shall overcome at last in a glorious manner. Verily, *no weapon that is formed against the church shall prosper.* Christ laughs at all the confederacies and plots, and mad rage of the world against his interest and members (Psalm 2:4). And his people (that are at present in a sad and sorrowful condition in the heat of the engagement) shall laugh too, and triumph over all. Martin Luther was very excellent in his expressions to this purpose. "That the kings and princes and people do so rage against the Lord and his Christ, I account (Luther says) an happy omen, and much better than if they fawned and flattered. For it follows (in the second psalm) he that *sitteth in the heavens shall laugh at them. Hoc autem principe nostro illos ridente, non video cur nobis fleadum sit a facie illorum.* As long as our king laughs at them, I see no reason why we should cry for them."

Luther says, "They that make Christ laugh by their ridiculous opposition, should not make his people cry. Verily every believer has that in his heart (I mean the victorious all-conquering grace of faith) whose prerogative it is to laugh to scorn all the foolish plots, and ill contrived designs, and feeble attempts of men against Christ and his church. For indeed their wise contrivances are foolishness, and their strongest endeavors against the impregnable and invincible interest of Christ and his church, are weakness itself, and will appear so at last. And if Christ laughs at them, why should not his friends and followers also?"

"For he laughs (as Luther goes on) not for his own, but for our sake, that we also through faith may laugh at the vain counsels of men."

There is need of faith, that the cause of faith may not be managed without faith, *ne causa fidei sit sine fide*. He that is sure of victory may well laugh in the face of his enemies. Now though wicked men are plowing and making long furrows on the backs of the righteous, yet the Lord will certainly cut down their works. The blessed Lord Jesus leads and assists his people, and the shout of a king and general is among them, (Num. 23:21), and that is assurance enough of victory. What an invincible army must the body of saints and believers necessarily be, of which not only the general, but *every* private soldier is invincible? They shall say at last, lo this is our God, we have waited for him, and he has saved us: this is the Lord, we have waited for him, and now we will be glad and rejoice in his salvation, *when all Moabs shall be trodden down as straw for the dunghill*, (Isaiah 25:9-10). O beloved! Lift up your heads and hands and be encouraged. Though it is a day of trouble and perplexity and of doubtful expectations in many respects, yet in the eye of faith it is a hopeful time and a promising season, when the world (this blind and mad world) is in a tumult and uproar against the church of Christ. The great and glorious things that are to be fulfilled, the faithful and true sayings of God cannot be accomplished by the quietness and sitting still of the nations. When the world rages against the church, and is up in arms to make havoc of it, then Christ Jesus, and those veteran legions, the glorious angels, the Lord Jesus, the man on the red horse among the myrtle trees, attended with red, speckled and white horses, angels deputed to several offices and administrations, (Zech. 1:8), are in a posture of readiness to charge the enemy, and bring off the people of God with safety and honor, that are hotly engaged in the conflict with their adversaries. The witnesses may be overcome and killed, but they shall live again. They that mourn for Jerusalem (*i.e.* the church), shall have a time to rejoice for her, and with her, (Isa. 66:10). Men that wage war against heaven, and bid open defiance to the great interest of the Lord Jesus (who is faithful and true, and in righteousness does judge and make war; who is king of kings, and Lord of Lords, (Rev. 19:11, *etc.*). Such wicked people shall be confounded, and Jerusalem shall be a burdensome stone and a cup of trembling to its adversaries. Indeed, we must wait on Christ's time for the exerting of his power, and the lighting down of his omnipotent array, during the day of his power and wrath, when he shall gird his sword on his thigh, and his arrows shall be sharp in the heart of his enemies. He shall thrash through the loins of those that rise up against him, and of them that hate him, that they rise not again. There is a day coming when the right hand of Christ shall teach him terrible things, (Psalm 45:4). In the meanwhile our work is to wait and pray, and exercise faith and patience (for here, or in this matter is the faith and patience of the saints proved and exercised) and when the day comes which God has determined, your very General alone can win the field, and turn the battle, and give you a signal victory. And he will do it very early for his suffering servants, that shall need to do nothing then, but stand still, and see the salvation of the Lord, and what destructions he will make among their adversaries. If one saint is in this way victorious (as you have heard) never question but the whole body of them shall (in God's time and way) prevail and conquer in a glorious manner.

Use 4.

Of exhortation to such as have believed through grace; in several branches.

1. Be encouraged then to fight this good fight, where there is so much hope, no such assurance to believers of a glorious victory. They must necessarily conquer that fight on such terms as we have mentioned, and have such provision laid in for victory and triumph. They must necessarily conquer, whose very General alone, is able to conquer all their enemies. Well may the Christian soldier be hardy, daring, venturous, courageous and resolute in his way to see on his enemies, that has such assurance of being triumphantly successful in all his engagements. Here is encouragement enough, one would think, to make any coward valiant in fight. Never despair nor give in then, but fight this good fight of faith.

Chapter 3: Uses of the Doctrine

First Branch of Exhortation in Ten Directions

1. Let all believers know and consider well that they are soldiers, and have fighting work before them. That they have many foes to deal with, and that they are in the field deeply engaged in a sharp contest about the things of their peace. And that there is no retreating, or drawing off, or looking back without shame and misery. That they are waging a war, that is of greatest importance, of everlasting consequence, and of infinite concern to them. Do not rest in slight apprehensions, transient and overly thoughts of your state and condition in this respect; in case you fall into a lavish like frame, (Judges 18:27), where you dwell securely and carelessly in the world, and expose yourselves to the inroads and inclusions of your enemies. Know that you do not dwell far from evil neighbors. You have mortal enemies bordering on you, that will make all advantage of your security. You have a troublesome, quarrelsome in-mate, one that was bred and born with you, and has grown up with you, and is a constant lodger in your house, and companion at home and abroad. Indwelling sin (I mean) with its confederates, that hold exact intelligence one to another, and watch all the advantages against you.

2. Labor to get accurate intelligence of the policies and designs of your adversaries. Acquaint yourselves with the deceitfulness of sin, the frauds and

impostures of the world, the wiles, methods, depths and advantages of the devil, the desperate wickedness of the heart, and the deep waters of evil counsel there. Find out the cabinet counsels and political design of your enemies against you. What they design, what stratagems they use, what advantageous seasons they choose to fight you in, what false colors they put out, that they may surprise you in the disguise of friends, what political retreats they make, what ambushes they lay, what reserves of fresh forces they have in readiness, what gradual and secret approaches they make, where they plant their artillery, and are designing to make a breach in your graces or comforts, that they may storm your soul, and make themselves masters of everything. Do what you can to inform yourselves what it is they drive at, how and where, and which way they are likely to assault you. In waging of war there is (as one speaks) the greatest improvement of humane wisdom and industry. Discover as much as may be the subtleties and policies, and forces and advantages of your enemies, that you may be provided to remove and avoid them.

    3. Get skill and dexterity in using the arms and weapons of your spiritual warfare. How to put on the girdle of truth, and breastplate of righteousness. How to use the shield of faith, and helmet of hope, and to wield the sword of the Spirit, (which is the word of God), and to improve all the pieces of your spiritual armor, and all the weapons that your general puts into your hands. A Christian is completely armed and appointed, but many

times does not know how to use his weapons. Have your arms in readiness, and learn to make a ready and dexterous use of them. That you should not only have grace, but be well skilled in the vigorous, lively, seasonable acting and exercising of all the grace you have, is the meaning of this direction.

4. List yourselves into some particular company that is engaged in the same warfare. It is a great disadvantage to a Christian to stand and fight alone, and not to have a particular and peculiar interest in the help of other Christians, which is the case of those that live out of church-fellowship, and do not put themselves under the watch and discipline, and conduct of particular churches. We (Solomon says, declaring the inconveniency of solitariness) to him that is alone, *when he falleth, for he has not another to help him up,* and if one prevail against him (that has a companion and helper) two shall withstand him, (Eccl. 4:10-12). It is as true in spiritual things as in civil and common cases. It is a great advantage in our spiritual conflicts to have good company, whose help and assistance is engaged to us. It is the Lord's appointment that mankind should live together in societies, as in families, commonwealths, churches, in order to have common helpfulness. It is the singular privilege of church members to have a peculiar engaged interest in the prayers, and counsels, and help of their fellow-brethren, which is a very desirable thing, and a considerable advantage, (1 Cor.

12:25-26). Do not therefore combat alone, but get into some particular body of the *saints militant*.

    5. Keep order. Fight everyone in your own places where you are set. Be sure you keep rank and file. Order is the beauty of the world, and of an army in special (in allusion to which the stars are frequently called the host of heaven, because of the exactness of their order and regular motion) and of the Christian army (the church of Christ in its militant condition) most of all. Of the spouse of Christ, it is said, "thy cheeks are comely with rows of jewels, (Song 1:10), that is, the outward face and countenance of the church is comely, beautiful and glorious with keeping their right place and order, as well as the manner of God's own ordinances, as some expound it. A church well-ordered is beautiful as Tirzah, comely as Jerusalem, and terrible to her adversaries as an army with banners, marching, led and ordered under their banners and ensigns (Song 6:4ff). This order is one respect in which churches are compared well to armies that are well ordered and disciplined. This is the glory and strength of such Christian societies, and no small advantage to every Christian. Those are the best soldiers that are best exercised to keep their own place and order. So, material a thing it is, that it is the character and description of good soldiers, that they were such as could keep rank, (1 Chron. 12:33, 36, 38). The private soldier must not straggle, or leave his place, or thrust himself into the place and command of the officer, but everyone must keep the place assigned him. A soldier

that is commanded to stand such a ground, must not leave it, even if he is sure to die in that place. If he leaves it, he dies for it by martial law. No personal danger will excuse him for such a breach of order. There is no dispensing with it. A Christian soldier must not be one that does not keep his place if I may so render it, nor one that breaks orders, and behaves disorderly. Rules of order must be carefully attended. Many of you see the beauty, and acknowledge the benefit of order in other societies, and observe it with much exactness at your trainings and artillery exercises, and must do so in real engagements. And why should not Christians apprehend the same necessity of attending order (Christ's order I mean) in every Christian army, every ecclesiastical society, and the same inconveniences of the contrary?

6. Maintain peace and union with your fellow-soldiers, or with those of the same company, or regiment, or army, as much as in you lies. Communion is what I mean with the members of the church in which you stand, and with the rest of the churches of Christ. There are some cases in which peace with men cannot be kept; no, in which it is a duty to contend against them earnestly for the faith, for the truth, for the glory of God, and for the good of the public. "But if it is possible, as much as lies in you (as for as it is possible, lawful and expedient) live peaceably with all men," (Rom. 12:18). Especially seek and follow peace with your fellow soldiers, your brethren and companions in tribulation,

and in the kingdom and patience of Jesus Christ. Peace among and mutual communion of churches and church-members is as necessary a thing, as peace and union in an army. I wish with all my soul that this might be attended in this great town of Boston. That these three churches might be as a threefold cord, so twisted together, that they might not be easily broken. Mutinies in an army between one company, or regiment, and another, are hazardous to the safety and good of the whole, and therefore severely punished. A wise general will correct that in his ranks, because it is a dangerous thing for the army. Christ, your General, is as apprehensive and jealous of such things among his people. Woeful was the case of Jerusalem, when besieged by the Romans on this account of divided parties and factions within, which hastened their ruin, and facilitated the Roman conquest. And do you think that divisions in and among churches are not of threatening consequence to such societies? May the Lord be merciful to us in this respect. Must the sword devour forever? Do you not know that it will be bitterness in the latter end? I hope you do not wage here an irreconcilable war. If the sons of men should be implacable, yet one would think the sons of God should put on (as the elect of God, holy and beloved) bowels of mercies, kindness, humbleness of mind, meekness, long-suffering, forbearing one another, and forgiving, if any man have a quarrel against any, as they expect forgiveness from the Lord Jesus, putting on charity, which is the bond of perfectness," (Col. 3:12-14). Shall that of the apostle, speaking of the worst of the heathen, (Rom. 1:31) be verified in any of the professors among us, that they are implacable, God forbid. They are your enemies, yes, common enemies to the interest of Christ, and his people that will go about to foment these divisions, or advise to the perpetuating of these differences. If I were not well assured that Christ's name, and interest, and your own souls suffer unspeakably by this, I should not have opened my mouth in this manner. However, I hope none here are so much in love with contention as to be angry with counsels of peace. It is a matter of great consequence. O! let us not turn our swords into one another's bowels, as the Midianites (Judges 7:22), Philistines (1 Sam. 14:15, 20), Moabites, Ammonites and the inhabitants of Mount Seir (2 Chron. 20:23), as well as others, have done to their own destruction. I believe, really that it is with these churches, or companies of Christian soldiers in this place, so far as there is any contention among them, as it is with soldiers now and then in the heat of battle. Sometimes through mistake in the hurry and confusion of battle, one regiment or company charges another of the same army, slaughtering and destroying their own dear friends, engaged on the same side, and for the same cause, instead of their enemies. This has occasioned great mischief. So, through darkness, confusions, misunderstandings, and misrepresentations of people and actions in an hour of temptation, it comes to pass that brethren contend and quarrel, and wound one another with the wound of an enemy, and of a cruel one. Mistakes and mis-apprehensions are the usual, sad occasions of great divisions. We have need to watch and pray, that we enter not into temptation in this respect, and to exercise charity towards such as differ from us in circumstances in only matters of doubtful disputation; otherwise we blindly run over and ruin, hack and hew down our friends and brothers under the notion of enemies. O! make and maintain peace among yourselves, you soldiers and military companies of Jesus Christ for a cessation of arms for the present is not enough. It is a league of amity and friendship, and brotherly communion that I contend for. O! that it might be speedily effected! Otherwise a common enemy will prove the only effectual mediator between the brethren at variance, and a pacification be made at last by such instruments and means as neither party will have any joy or pleasure in. And the blessing of the peace-maker be on the heads of those persons that shall be graciously instrumental in Gods way to settle a good and lasting peace and correspondence among these churches, or sincerely and vigorously endeavor it.

7. Make it your chief care and business all the time of your warfare to please your great General the Lord of hosts, the Lord Jesus Christ in all things. That is the property of a good soldier, (2 Tim. 2:4). He designs to please his Commander in Chief, by a ready obedience. This was the singular commendation of the centurion

soldiers, (Matt. 8:9; Luke 7:8). No men are under more absolute command then soldiers, that must not dispute, but obey the orders of their general. In like manner do you observe all the orders of the Lord Jesus, obey all his words of command, adventure on the hottest and hardest pieces of service, when he requires it; hold no intelligence, or treacherous, close correspondence with his enemies. In every motion or action consider with yourselves whether this or that course, and carriage and posture will please Christ. And in particular please him by a ready and cheerful obedience to inferior, commissioned officers for his sake. "Obey them that have the rule over you," is one great word of command which our Lord and Savior gives, (Heb. 13: 7, 17). Though I am as truly and heartily opposite to the Presbyterian persuasion[7] (with due respect to the piety and learning, and orthodoxy and excellent abilities and accomplishments of those our fellow-brethren, and soldiers that march on that side of the way, as it is spoken) in which it lies in direct opposition to the substantials of the congregational-way of government, as many of you know. And though I am remote enough from the intention of improving the text but now mentioned, to the establishing of such an absolute and arbitrary rule in the presbytery, as is really inconsistent, and incompatible with the due privilege and liberty of the people, yet, I am sure that all are not guides, overseers, and rulers, but that there are rulers and ruled,

---

[7] Oaks was an independent. – Editor.

the governors and the governed in all particular churches according the sovereign institution of Jesus Christ. There are officers and private soldiers according to the appointment of our Lord General. And I must say freely, that that way of church-government that does not allow the rule, and government truly and properly so called, to church officers, is not the way of Christ's institution. Obey therefore such as the Lord Jesus has set over you in the Lord, if you mean to please him. Otherwise you may be sure that your General will severely punish the undue contempt of the meanest officer in the Christian army.

8. Be willing to endure hardship. This is another qualification of a soldier, (2 Tim. 2:3). Church-officers are called to this in a special manner: but it is the duty also, of every Christian soldier, that must expect to wrestle with many difficulties. A man must never think to be a soldier that is nice and delicate, and loves to favor himself and indulges to pleasure and ease. Tertullian said that every soldier must resolve upon enduring, hunger, and thirst, and cold, and wet, and weariness, and lying upon the ground, many hardships and inconveniences in the course of his military employment. As Alcas the scythian said to Philip of Macedon, "You command Macedonians that can fight with men; but I command Scythians that are able to fight with hunger and thirst." A course of warfare is usually a course of hardship, as well. Christians must look for many hardships in their way, ill-usage, difficult times,

sore inconveniencies, and hard duty in their warfare. It is their great wisdom and duty to expect them, and learn to deal faithfully with them.

9. Do not encumber yourselves with other occasions, or with anything that may take you off, or hinder you in your warfare. "No man that warreth entangleth himself with the affairs of this life," (2 Tim. 2:4). Soldiers are greatly taken off from other employments; they cannot follow merchandizing or farming, or this or that trade to any great purpose while they are soldiers. They have enough to do to attend their watchings and wardings, marchings and motions, the orders and commands of their leaders. It is true that a particular calling is very well consistent with the general calling of a Christian soldier, and should be so attended and managed, that it may be a furtherance and no hindrance to it. But may we not fear that there is a fault among Christian soldiers in this respect? And that they are generally too much engaged in other matters, and entangled with the world and its affairs, and by it rendered less disposed to the service of Christ in their Christian warfare. Certainly, inordinate affection to the things of this world, and over eager pursuit of them in no way creates a good soldier of Christ.

10. Be content with your wages, that is the good quality of a soldier, as John the Baptist intimates, (Luke 3:14). A Christian properly has no wages, because all he enjoys is of mere grace and courtesy. When he has done all, he is an unprofitable servant, (Luke 17:10). But my

meaning is, be contented with what the Lord Jesus Christ affords you at present for your sustenance and encouragement. Yes, though he keep you at shore allowance as to comforts and spiritual suavities, and such a sufficiency of grace to prevail, and conquer, and tread down all your enemies, as you could desire; yet be quiet and contented with your present portion; do not bring a mutiny or murmur, but be humbly thankful for, and well sufficed with such things as you have, (Heb. 13:5). And be assured that the Lord Jesus, though he owes you nothing, and keeps you short at present, will pay you well at last. The time is coming, when you shall be drawn out of the field, and discharged from this warfare, and then he will pay you all your arrears, over and over, and gratify you for all your service (such is his grace) with that which you may comfortably subsist on to eternity.

    This is the first branch of the exhortation. Let all true believers be greatly encouraged to fight against their spiritual enemies; and that both in their private and public capacities. For every believer must engage in a warfare, not only general and common to all Christians, but also proper and peculiar to himself in his place and condition. Therefore, I would crave leave to address myself here with a word or two of encouragement to our pious, faithful, honorable rulers in their stations, not as they are only Christians, but as they are also Christian magistrates, and the nursing fathers of our common-wealth and churches.

Chapter 3: Uses of the Doctrine

It would indeed be a most importune and intolerable thing, notorious boldness and rudeness in me this day, and on such an occasion, to stand here and dictate to our honorable patriots and worthies, or to direct and advise them about the particular management of their civil affairs. As every man should be wise in his own calling and concerns. So it is the great happiness of New-England that we have persons of great worth and wisdom, integrity and experience, ruling over us, and guiding us by the skillfulness of their hands; and such as have no need of the instructions of such a piece of weakness and unworthiness as stands before you. They know their own business, and are taught of God to manage the great affairs under their hands. I remember well, that I am an unworthy minister of the gospel; not a statesman, or projector. And therefore, I am very fair from the design of obtruding upon you (much honored by raw and indigested apprehensions about the condition of your affairs, and what may seem counselable in that respect. But I would with all fidelity, respect and affection, administer to you a word of encouragement, in an application of what has been discoursed of the Christians warfare in general to your warfare in special.

You must combat with profaneness, with turbulent difficulties, with blasphemies, with injustice, with disorders of many kinds. And in doing so you will be exposed to difficult and hard speeches, yes, to many hardships and discouragements, and if you should be ready sometimes to quit in this public office, and complain that you are not able to bear this heavy burden that is laid on you, it would be no more then what we read of Moses, the meekest man, and one of the best accomplished leaders and governors that ever was on earth, (Num. 11:11-14). The eminency of your place and work makes you more conspicuous, that you will be the fairest mark for Satan and his instruments. Satan and his followers, that fight under his banner, will be casting all their darts at you.

Magistrate's places are as furnaces to try them in. The place of government tries the spirit of a man, whether he is just or corrupt, liberal or covetous, valiant or fearful, for God or for man. As Mr. Cotton observes in Eccl. 3:18–22, every calling has its temptation. And yours (as high and honorable as it is) is not privileged in that respect. You are *gods* indeed in the manner in which scripture describes you (Psalm 82:1, 6). But you are men too, subject to the same passions, perturbations, conflicts and temptations, that other men are. No more exposed to it on some accounts. Your places are high, and you dwell in the upper region; but you are wiser then to look for nothing but stillness and serenity there, where you are not out of the way and walk of the prince of the power of the air, who will be sure (if he can) to raise many a storm and tempest on you. I am not very acquainted with the state of your affairs. But if I should improve my observations and conjecture from what I have noted elsewhere, I might well conclude, that you have more than enough difficulties before you in your way. You are continually travailing in birth with the public good; and there may be some that (as it is said of the dragon, that he stood before the woman that was ready to be delivered, to devour her child as soon as it was born, Rev. 12:4), so, will be ready to stifle the issues of your counsels as they are birthed, or to overlay them, and reroute them as soon as they are born. Now the word of the Lord to you is (as sometimes to Joshua, (Joshua 1:9)), "be strong and of a good courage, be not afraid, neither be you dismayed, for the Lord your God is with you." O! take courage and acquit yourselves as the good soldiers of Christ, and valiant worthies, in your warfare. You have growing sins in a growing commonwealth to grapple with. O! be courageous, and fight your fight against such enormities. Do not draw your sword merely to flourish and beat the air; but strike home. And if you do not have swords that are sharp enough, or long enough to reach, to do thorough execution on the enemies of our peace, the God-provoking and state disturbing sins and evils among us, be sure you get such as may do it. I refer to and mean such laws as may be keen and comprehensive enough to reach them. And the Lord bless you, (with the honored deputies) at your great council of war, as I would take liberty, they describe your general assembly, where you are considering what to do to conquer and beat down the sins and disorders that lift up their head among us, and are the great enemies of the prosperity of our commonwealth and churches.

I might also particularly apply this word of encouragement to the pious and laborious servants of the Lord in the work of the ministry. Oh my brethren and fathers! You are the good soldiers of Jesus Christ in a peculiar manner, (2 Tim. 2:3). Paul calls Epaphroditus the pastor of the church of the Philippians, his fellow-soldier, (Phil. 2:25). Both extraordinary and ordinary church-officers are soldiers. Your life is a warfare in a way of specialty. Besides the enemies you have to engage with as you are Christians, you have enemies also to conflict with as you are ministers. I do not speak of the people of men which are to be pitied and tendered, but of their vices, which must be opposed and combated with it. You have unruliness, disorderly behavior, prejudices, reproaches, base nick-names, hard usage, and injurious dealings among men; the pride, ignorance, obstinacy, unfruitfulness, and ingratitude of some you have to do with, besides your particular temptations from Satan (who maligns the ministers of Christ more than other men) to conflict and combat with it. Some of you may be in Paul's case, fears within, and fightings without, and trouble on every side, (2 Cor. 7:5). You are soldiers and must expect knocks and blows in your warfare. But you may be assured of a most glorious victory. We live in times of great degeneracy, and especially of great disaffection to the ministers of Christ. Times in which Satan industriously instills and infuses endless jealousies and prejudices into the heads and hearts of people concerning the faithful ministers of the gospel. As the king of Syria said to his captains, fight neither with small nor great, save only with the king of Israel, (1 Kings 22:31), so Satan seems to say to his followers at this day. Do you fight neither with one another, so much as with the ministers of Christ? This is the ball that Satan has at his foot, the great game that he is playing, up and down; to asperse, and vilify, and bring down the price and esteem of Christs messengers as well knowing, then, how to destroy the souls of men and women, heaps upon heaps, as it were. Well, you are soldiers, and must not be discouraged. You are well appointed; you have arms to fight with. Prayers and tears and ministerial authoritative dispensation of the word and ordinances of Christ, with courage and undaunted resolution, are the weapons of your warfare, which are not carnal, but spiritual and mighty through God assisting, (2 Cor. 10:4). And if it would not sound too much like the word of a commander, if it were not too much boldness and arrogance, I would say to my reverend fathers and brethren, fellow soldiers stand to your arms. The day is your own, and the victory will be finally determined on your side. Your sighs, and groans, and prayers, and tears, and conflict shall not be in vain; but the Lord will shortly give you the victory. Take heed of short-spiritedness, of impatience, of fainting in the contest, though it may be sharp and severe for a time. The libertarian spirit, the anti-ministerial spirit, the heretical evil spirit, the disorderly spirit, or whatever else it is that you combat with shall be routed, run down, put to flight; and the folly of such things and people will be made manifest to all men. Nothing will abide, but what is built, not on the variable and uncertain fancies and affections of men, but on, the everlasting foundations of scripture and reason. Reason and truth will stand their ground and keep the field when all that is opposite to it will be put to flight and totally discomfited.

I shall say no more to you but in the words of the Lord to the prophet, Jer. 1:18-19, "The Lord hath made you defensed cities, iron pillars, and brazen walls; and though men fight against you they shall not prevail; for the Lord is with you."

No, further, if I could but get into the hearts of any of the people of God in this assembly, and make discovery of the particular corruptions and temptations that this or that believing man or woman is conflicting and combating with; I would say to them, be strong in the Lord, and in the power of his might. As the priests were ordered by the Lord to give a word of encouragement to the people of Israel, when they were approaching to battle against their enemies, (Deut. 20:3-4), so give me leave at the head of this Christian camp here assembled before the Lord, to speak to the Israel of God, and to say, let not your hearts faint, fear not, and do not tremble, neither be terrified, because of your enemies. For the Lord your God (even your great Lord

General, the Lord Jesus Christ) is he that goes with you to fight for you against your enemies, and to save you. What should I do but say to them that are of a fearful heart, be strong, fear not: strengthen your weak hands, and confirm feeble knees, (Isa. 35:3-4)? You are, it may be, buffeted with Satan's messenger, pained with the thorn in the flesh, molested and tortured (as people held upon the rack) with temptations to atheism, and unbelief, with blasphemous injections, and amazing suggestions, tormented with the poisonous fiery darts and arrows of that evil one, combated with fleshly, worldly lusts and corruptions that give you no rest. O! courage, courage, dear hearts, fight it out to the last. And if you are foiled, get up again by repentance, and renew the combat in the strength of Christ, and never ask half-heartedly, or make a surrender of yourselves to the will of your enemies; for you shall obtain a glorious victory.

Possibly (Oh believer) you have been sleeping in the lap of some Delilah, and have lost your strength, and are given into the hands of the Philistine, that have bound you with chains, and made you to grind (which is the sad condition which some Christian soldiers, through security, reduce themselves to). Yet, let me tell you for your encouragement, that though your locks are shaven off, yet (through grace) the locks of your strength will grow again, and you shall cast off those Philistines. Let all the followers of Christ be warned by the falls and surprises of themselves and others to stand on their guard, and continue in a vigilant fighting posture, that they may not give up themselves to the will of their adversaries, that lie in ambush, and watch all advantages against them. "Watch ye, stand fast in the faith; quit you like men, be strong," (1 Cor. 16:13). Yet a little while, and you shall triumph over all your enemies. The Lord will shortly deliver you from sin and sorrow, and the sores of an evil world, and bruise Satan under your feet, (Rom. 16:20). The God of peace shall do it for you, when the time of your warfare shall be accomplished.

Second Branch of Exhortation

So much for the first branch of the exhortation. The second is learn and labor to improve the Lord Jesus Christ in all your spiritual conflicts and engagements. For lack of this holy skill men do but beat the air, and make a vain flourish; and contend to no purpose at all with the enemies that war against their souls. Here all the false religions in the world, and that of the papists especially, fail exceedingly. They are wholly unacquainted with the mystery of the gospel, the efficacy of the performances of Jesus Christ, the orderly way of improving the satisfaction, merit and intercession, or the humiliation and exaltation of the Mediator, *etc.* And what course do they fix on? Truly they think to vanquish their corruptions in the strength of their voices and fastings and penances, and self-devised, self-lacerating austerities; which may possibly kill the natural man, but will never destroy the corrupt old man. And to frighten away Satan (the tame and timorous devil) with their crossings and holy-water, and such like Popery. That which lies at the bottom of all their miscarriages in this business is, that they do not know how to improve the Lord Jesus in order to defeat and overthrow of their spiritual adversaries. Without this divine skill men may scuffle and skirmish with their foes, raise much dust, and make a great noise and bustle, as if they would do great exploits, and yet they all end in shame and disappointment.

So, you see that all the victories and conquests which believers obtain are through him that loved them; even the Lord Jesus Christ. O! therefore increase that spiritual art of improving the Lord Jesus in all your combat, and never do nothing. Much should have been said here about that fullness of provision that is laid up in Jesus Christ for the support, relief and assistance of believers in their conflicts, and their enablement to make a conquest of their enemies. Or about the actings of faith on the Lord Jesus, and seeking in all suitable and seasonable supplies of strength and grace from his store. Time and strength would fail me, if I should enter on so large and spacious a subject; and I had rather say nothing, then speak generally, superficiality, and slightly to a matter of such importance; therefore, I shall in this way pass it with a brief mention of it.

Third Branch of Exhortation

Acknowledge the love of God in Christ, and bless the God and Father of our Lord Jesus Christ for all your partial and present victories and conquests in any of your engagements with the enemies of your souls. Does the Lord help you to acquit yourselves like men or like *Christians* rather, and the soldiers of Jesus Christ in any conflicts with your own corruptions, or Satan's temptations? O! remember that it is through the love of God in Christ that you prevail and conquer. And therefore, bless God and be thankful to him for all your victorious achievements, and offer him the sacrifice of praise and thanksgiving. When Jehoshaphat and his people went forth against that great multitude of Moabites, Ammonites, and the inhabitants of Mount Seir with full assurance from the Lord of victory; singers to the Lord were appointed, that should praise the beauty of holiness. And they went out before the army, and said, "praise the Lord, for his mercy endureth forever," (2 Chron. 20:21). They met the enemy with thanksgiving in their mouths for promised and assured victory. And when their enemies were overthrown in a wonderful manner, they assembled in the valley of Berachah, so called, because they *blessed* the Lord there. They returned to Jerusalem with psalteries, and harps and trumpets to the house of the Lord, (verses 26-28). In the same manner believers have assurance from the Lord of the utter defeat and overthrow, and of the absolute conquest of their foes through the love of God in Christ; and may well go forth against their enemies in the strength of the Lord, with the high praises of God in their mouth, and a two edged sword in their hand, even the sword of the Spirit, the word of God, that is sharper than a two edged sword, and will not fail, if it is rightly managed, to do notable execution. And when they obtained any signal victory in this or that particular engagement with their spiritual enemies, what should they do but give the name of Berachah, their rest and places of retirement, and bless the Lord and his holy name (in which they are to set up their banners (Psalm 20:5), and through which they have done valiantly, and trodden down all their enemies, (Psalm 119:118), with their souls and all that is within them. Though you cannot in this life hope for the total defeat and overthrow of the enemies of your souls, yet be sure to erect a trophy, and rear up a monumental pillar of thankful acknowledgement and remembrance to the power and grace and love of God in Christ, on every partial and particular victory you obtain in the field against them.

Fourth Branch of Exhortation

Lastly, wait, and pray, and look, and long for that glorious day, when your warfare shall be ended, and you shall go out of the field victorious, and triumphant, as absolute conquerors. I do not persuade you to participate in any impatience during the heat of your present engagements. Take heed of tiring and fainting in your conflicts, and in the laborious course of your warfare: though your general part you are on hard duty and service. *He that looks for mastery is not crowned, except he serves lawfully,* Calvin judiciously says. Something done lawfully is to hold on the contest, or continue and persevere in the conflict, as long as the law prescribes. No man is to give over before the time appointed. He that is tired with a first or second conflict, and withdraws himself out of the field before his time; will lose his crown. Perseverance in a course of running and wrestling, and combating, with patience, and submission to the good will of God, is the duty of every Christian. But with it, it is the duty, as well as allowance, of the followers of Christ, to have respect to the recompence of reward, and the joy that is set before you. And to wait (with hope and desire) all the days of their *warfare* (as the original has it) or when their change comes, (Job 14:14). That happy great change, when their present warfare shall be changed into everlasting peace and rest from trouble, and their helmets shall be changed into crowns of everlasting joy on their heads, and their swords and spears (not beaten into plow-shares and pruning-hooks, as Isa. 2:4), but changed into palms in their hands in token of assured victory and triumph. O! therefore let all Christian soldiers love and long for the glorious appearance of Christ.

And when you are beset and encumbered, and engaged in any hot dispute with your enemies, look upwards, and sigh to heaven, as for present assistance and enablement, so also, for after perfect deliverance, victory and triumph, which shall be brought to you at the appearing of the Lord Jesus Christ.

 With this word I should have concluded and issued the whole discourse and put an end to the present engagement. But that I conceive it may be rationally expected that I should address myself in the close (in a word or two at least) to the military men, the worthy and much honored gentlemen, that have pressed and called me forth to the service of this day. I do not need to tell you that I am no soldier. Possibly my intent to use some military and martial phrases in the past discourse may but too plainly show you, that I am but little acquainted with the military science or faculty. I am no friend to war, but an unfeigned lover of peace. I long for an end of war and blood-sheds, the destructions and desolations that the poor world is filled with. O! when will this way expire, and that glorious morn appear, that lightsome day dawn, in which the nations shall beat their swords into plough-shears, and their spears into pruning-hooks, and no more shall nation lift up sword against nation, neither shall they learn war anymore?

 The God of peace will certainly put an end unto these wars, but in the meantime it is the wisdom and duty of the people of God to improve all advantages that are providentially put into their hands, to secure their peace and precious enjoyments, and to put themselves into a posture and condition of disputing it with those that may invade or assault them. Military skill is necessary in military times and martial days; and these military exercises are not only lawful and allowable, but laudable, yes, and necessary also. And the people by whom they are supported and carried on deserve singular commendation and encouragement. David's marvelous and mighty men are catalogued in holy Scripture, as men of renown and worthy to be had in honorable remembrance. And surely the gentlemen among us that are men of skill and conduct, and experts in military affairs should not be slighted or discouraged. We live in times of great commotions and doubtful expectations. How long we may sit under our vines and fig-trees and have none to make us afraid, the God of our peace, our great Protector, only knows. The day may come on us, when we may wish there were many more worthy men of martial spirits and military accomplishments, then yet appear among us.

 It is true, that I have not directed my discourse to the soldiers this day, considering that I was not (unless I mistook my summons) to make a military oration (which is more proper for some gentleman of that profession) but to preach a sermon, on a military occasion, that might be of use (if the Lord please) to the whole assembly. I have weakly, but designedly endeavored to imitate and tread in the steps of our blessed Savior, the Captain of our salvation, (Heb. 2:10), with whom it was usual and customary in the days of his converse on earth, to take the least hint to make a spiritual use and advantage of common things, and to improve obvious occasions and occurrences in a parabolical, allegorical, and spiritual way. In the same manner I have taken rise and advantage from the military occasions of this day to discourse (as the Lord has enabled of the spiritual and Christian warfare. Soldiers love to hear of battles at land or sea, of victories and triumphs, and the consequences of it, the spoils, the plunder, the booty, the regards of gallantry and good behavior in such engagements. And I have been acquainting you with such things in a spiritual way. And I hope none of you will judge this wholly impertinent, unless you have so far put on the artillery man this morning, that you have also put off the Christian soldier.

I shall say further (by way of defense and apology) that what I have discussed may be of great use to the gentlemen I am speaking to in their military capacity. That which conduces to making men good in this has a general influence into the due department of men in all capacities. That man that has conquered and subdued himself will know how to command, how to obey, much better than one that is a slave to himself, and his own perverse will, and in bondage to his own lusts and corruptions. Such a man will give serious and conscionable attendance to the improvement of all means afforded him, that may accomplish him in a military way, and furnish him with skill and dexterity, by which he may be enabled to fight the Lord's battles against injurious and malignant adversaries. He will depend on that God that teaches his hands to war, and his fingers to fight, (Psalm 144:1). He umpires or determines the successes and events of all military engagements according to the counsel of his own will, sometimes contrary to the law and common rule of second causes. So that, the battle is not always to the strong, but time and chance (some intervening providential occurrences) happens to this, as well as other affairs, (Eccl. 9:11). He will go forth, when God calls to the defense of civil and religious liberties in the strength of the Lord, and not in his own might or sufficiency, having had such sensible and instructing experience, that all his spiritual and greater conquests are acquired through him that loved him. He will be one of the thundering legion, that by their powerful and princely prayers will obtain signal victories over their enemies. He will be one of the called, and faithful, and chosen, that will follow the lamb wherever he leads them. He that (through the grace and strength of Christ) has conquered sin, and self, and Satan, and an evil world, and is sure to conquer his last enemy death (which is the happy condition of a Christian soldier). He will not fear the face of any man in a righteous cause, but have the spirit and courage, and undaunted resolution, of a soldier indeed. He will say, as Nehemiah in his case, (Neh. 6:11), "Should such a man as I flee?" Well may he be above fear and frights, and cowardice, and acquaint himself in all respects as a magnanimous person, who has deliverance from the fear of death, to the bondage of which all men are naturally subject, (Heb. 2:15). He that expects to gain by dying (as that champion Paul did, Phil. 1:21). And therefore, he does not fear to die, will not be afraid of the point of the sword or mouth of the canon, or any other instruments of death, when God calls him to adventure himself. If Alexander, Julius Caesar, and others worked such great things by their natural courage and valor, what will that man do that has the spirit and valor of a Christian soldier? He will not be acting to work pride, and ambition, and vain glory. He will not be after a mercenary spirit that other soldiers are carried with, but will bear on the greatness of his God, and the goodness of his care, and so jeopardize himself in the high places of the field. These and the same things considered, my discourse may not seem to be wholly foreign, or unaccommodable to the affairs of this day. Whether it has been proper to the design and business of the day is left to your judgement. But I am sure that I have discoursed of the best and most important warfare, and the most desirable and glorious victory. And though I cannot but approve and commend and wish the prosperous continuance of your trainings and artillery-exercises, yet behold (as Paul speaks in another case, 1 Cor. 12:31), I have been "shewing you a more excellent way."

    Of all soldiers, the Christian soldier is the best: no war, nor victory, nor triumph can be comparable to his. He is more than a soldier; more than a conqueror. And happy will that man be that at the end of his race, and when he is marching out of the field, shall be able to say (as that great apostle and renowned soldier of Jesus Christ, 2 Tim. 4:7-8), "I have fought a good fight, I have finished the course of my warfare: and henceforth there is laid up for me a crown of righteousness, which the Lord, the righteous judge, shall give me at the blessed day of his glorious appearing."

FINIS

Other Works on Spiritual Warfare at Puritan Publications

The Christian's Combat Against the Devil
by Christopher Love (1618-1651)

Are you ready for battle? Is the devil just a figment of your imagination? In the evil day will you stand firm? Do you have on the whole armor of God? What is your strategy for spiritual warfare?

A Comfort for the Afflicted Christian
by William Plumer (1802-1880)

How well do you handle trials? How well do you handle tribulation, depression, death in the family, the loss of a job, poor health, the loss of possessions, etc. Are you content? In this devotional work, Plumer aids the Christian by Scripture to overcome all these things and truly glorify God in our affliction.

The Armor of God
by Paul Bayne (1573-1617)

You are in a spiritual war if you are a professing Christian. Are you prepared for it? Paul Bayne teaches you how to wear God's armor for victory in Christ.

Walking Victoriously in the Power of the Spirit
by C. Matthew McMahon

Are you walking victoriously in the Spirit? Are you baptized by the Spirit, indwelt by the Spirit, walking abundantly in Jesus Christ by the Spirit? Do you even regularly talk this way?

Joseph's Resolve and the Unreasonableness of Sinning Against God
by C. Matthew McMahon

How much do you hate sin? Joseph was resolved to cast off all wickedness as he lived before the face of God. Do you?

A Discourse on the Damned Art of Witchcraft
by William Perkins (1558-1602)

Are you in league with Satan? Are you unknowingly in covenant with the devil? How affected is your house with superstition and witchcraft? You would be surprised! William Perkins delivers a valuable treatise on the subject.

Demonology and Theology
by Nathaniel Holmes (or Homes) (1599–1678)

Do you ever wish anyone good luck? Do you ever read the horoscopes? Nathaniel Holmes demonstrates biblically how the black arts of Satan have infiltrated the church, and how they ought to be combated through the power of the Holy Spirit. He shows in great detail the black arts of witchcraft and satanism, and the chapter on Astrology alone is worth the cost of the work.